RETURN TO KABUL

*Georg Taubmann's thrilling return
to Kabul after his captivity
and the rebuilding of the
Shelter Now Development Agency*

EBERHARD MÜHLAN
with GEORG TAUBMANN

35 Years of Shelter Now International
From its exciting beginnings up to the present

RETURN TO KABUL

© 2021 Eberhard Mühlan and Georg Taubmann

All rights reserved. No part of this publication may be reproduced, distributed, or transmitted in any form or by any means, including photocopying, recording, or other electronic or mechanical methods, without the prior written permission of the publisher, except in the case of brief quotations embodied in critical reviews and certain other noncommercial uses permitted by copyright law. For permission requests, write to the publisher, addressed "Attention: Permissions Coordinator," at the address below.

Publishers Solution, LLC
4954 Alamance Dr., SE
Southport NC 28461
www.PublishersSolution.com

Ordering Information:
   Quantity sales. Special discounts are available on quantity purchases by hospitals, doctor practices, corporations, associations, and others. For details, contact the publisher at the address above.
   Orders by U.S. trade bookstores and wholesalers. Please contact Publishers Solution:
Tel: (434) 944-5800 or visit www.PublishersSolution.com.
   Printed in the United States of America

MühlanMedien 1st edition
MühlanMedien www.MühlanMedien.de

ISBN 978-1-937925-31-4

Cover Design: Megan Dillon

Cover photo: Michael Miklas, www.michaelmiklas.com

Interior Design: Christopher Kirk

Contents

Introduction ix

We Are Going Back to Afghanistan! 1

In the Spotlight in Germany 5
    Review of the Year with Günther Jauch 6
    Reception by the Federal President in Schloss Bellevue. 8
    Press Scrums and Crisis Management in Germany. 9

Looking Back: Taken Hostage, Rescued 17
    Taken Hostage. 18
    Released in the Nick of Time! 29

Afghanistan—Focus of International Interest .45
    The First International Conference on Afghanistan 45
    Rise and Fall of the Taliban 48
    Looking Back: Bombs and Prayers 53

Return—Obstacles in the Way 65
    To Pakistan—Despite Entry Ban 66
    Staff Get-together in Swat 69
        Georg Hits Burnout 69
        Friends in Peshawar 72

Plans for Kabul 72
Looking Back: Before the Supreme Court 74
   Condemned under Sharia 75

Back in Kabul 91
Flashbacks and Ecstatic Joy 91
Looking Back: Remembering the Period of Captivity 94
Rejection and a Warm Welcome 111
Looking Back: In the Snare of the Religious Police 114
If Only a Car Could Speak 130
A New Home in Kabul 132
An Unexpected Test 133
The First Project in Shamalie 134
Shelter Now Women Return to Kabul 139

A Change in Family Life 145
Attack on the Boarding School in Pakistan 146
Involvement in Pakistan Increases 149
Marianne with the Boys in Germany 150
Interview with Daniel and Benjamin Taubmann 151
Georg Alone in Kabul—Years of Extensive Rebuilding 157
Attacks on Georg 161
Shelter Now International Office in Germany 163
The Years 2008-2018 163
   New Projects 163
   Work Under Increasingly Dangerous Conditions 166

35 Years of Shelter Now International 175
The Years 1979-1989 175
   Civil Wars and Floods of Refugees 175
   An Adventurous Journey to Pakistan 178
From 1988-1990 182
   Vandalism, Destruction, the End 182
   Return and New Beginning 186
From 1991-1993 187
   Gulf War and Threatening Letters 187
   Development projects in Afghanistan 190
   Rescued at the Last Moment 193

   Khairat, a Pashtun Celebration of Thanksgiving...................197
From 1994-2000...198
   From Mujahideen Terror to Taliban Terror.......................199
   Move to Kabul and Settling In 200
From 2001-2002...203
From 2003-2008...204
   Further development or projects in Afghanistan 204
From 2008-2014...205
From 2014-2018...206
   New Relief and Development work started in Northern Iraq (Kurdistan)..206

Endnotes 209

Introduction

Thousands have read the book *Escape from Kabul*, which documented the more than three months of imprisonment of eight Shelter Now International[1] Development Workers. The Taliban held them as hostages following the Al Qaeda terrorist attacks on the World Trade Center in New York on September 11, 2001. The workers were to be used in exchange for terrorists and in negotiations with the American forces during their acts of reprisal in Afghanistan. Their dramatic release by American Special Forces from the clutches of the Taliban was extremely risky.

"If God had not done so many miracles, we would not have come out alive," Georg Taubmann, leader of the team, explained later.

Shelter Now has been working for 35 years among Afghan refugees in Pakistan and Afghanistan. They help with primary care through the provision of food, drinking water and medical aid among the refugees. They built outpatient clinics, schools and thousands of mud houses for the Afghans who were streaming across the border into Pakistan in tens of thousands, and being accommodated in provisional refugee camps in desert-like areas by the Pakistan Government.

In 1983, Shelter Now first got involved in the primary care of refugees. Due to the Russian invasion in 1979 and the establishment of a Communist system in Afghanistan, hundreds of thousands of refugees poured across the border into

> God cannot be excluded from the life story of Georg Taubmann. His organization has always made it a rule to help everyone in need in Pakistan and Afghanistan, regardless of their religious or political affiliation.
>
> His life speaks volumes and reflects the command of Jesus, "Love the Lord your God with all your heart and with all your soul ... and your neighbor as yourself" (Matt. 22:37).
>
> Once after an event, a politician said, "By his commitment Mr. Taubmann has redefined the Christian faith!"
>
> It is fascinating how Georg brings God into his daily life, speaks with Him and listens to His instructions.

neighboring Pakistan. Years later Shelter Now looked after Afghans from the former Communist regime who had fled the Taliban regime in Afghanistan.

Shelter Now initially specialized in the construction of low-cost houses made of prefabricated concrete. Later they also built mud houses so that the refugees living in tents or under tarpaulins, could find relief from the burning heat.

Reconstruction projects for those returning to ruined villages in Afghanistan were added later.

Numerous times the Shelter Now staff found themselves facing life threatening attacks, kidnappings and other threatening situations. Twice their projects were totally demolished and materials plundered—first in 1990 by fanatical Islamists in Pakistan, second in 2001 by radical Taliban fighters in Afghanistan. Damages amounting to several million Euros forced the organization to close down; the foreign workers had to leave the country.

Both times Georg Taubmann began rebuilding the relief organization out of nothing, even while facing murder threats and kidnap attempts. His love for the suffering Afghan people and his deep faith allowed him no rest and drove him to achieve what many would consider humanly impossible.

In 2019, Shelter Now began its 36th year. The origins and the history of this organization read like a thrilling detective novel—except it is not fiction, but the real truth. This book chronicles the exciting beginnings of Shelter Now and trace its history chronologically.

This book is the continuation of the best seller *Escape from Kabul*. Only a few months after their dramatic liberation from the privations and dangers of their imprisonment, Georg Taubmann was already collecting a team and starting again in Afghanistan. Please read on. Allow yourself to be drawn into the thrilling account of Taubmann's return and the resurrection of projects others thought dead … despite renewed threats of kidnapping. Excerpts from the out-of-print book *Escape from Kabul* are included to explain the background.

We Are Going Back to Afghanistan!

After their dramatic liberation from the besieged city of Ghazni, the four German Shelter Now aid workers retained a resolute determination. Scarcely had they climbed out of the rescue helicopter and introduced themselves to the press at the German Embassy in Islamabad than they declared that they would return to Afghanistan as soon as possible. This was unexpected. The press were amazed … indeed irritated.

Their offices and projects in Afghanistan had largely been plundered. Even their personal belongings had been stolen by Taliban thugs. Their response? "We're going back and will carry on!" For more than three months they had been held as hostages in a series of makeshift prisons in Kabul under inhumane conditions, with their lives had constantly under threat. Yet they would rebuild their aid projects—despite the dangers. "Where do they get this courage and confidence from?" many wondered.

Georg Taubmann: Even during my time in prison it was clear to me that I would return to Afghanistan, if only we could manage to get out alive. In spite of all the terrible things which we observed and experienced, I felt extremely close to the Afghans – especially those who, like us, were in prison though innocent and were subject to dreadful mistreatment. After the dramatic release by American Special Forces on 15 November 2001 in Ghazni, we flew into Islamabad that morning by helicopter. That same evening there was the first press conference at the German Embassy. Press representatives from all around the world were present. I told them our story, beginning with the trap which was set by the Taliban Religious Police for two of our female American colleagues, the kidnapping of us eight Shelter Now workers, the accusation that we had converted Muslims, right up to our 103-day incarceration (the two American women were 105 days in prison) and the unexpected rescue. Finally, in the name of all the Germans who had been set free, I said that we all had the desire to return to Afghanistan as soon as possible.

Especially now that the Taliban had been overthrown, the devastated country would need as much help as possible to rebuild. I stressed also that we would forgive those who had wrecked our relief organization and done us so much evil. Of course we had been on an emotional rollercoaster and had had intermittent feelings of fear and hatred, but we were Christians and were prepared to forgive. Just as it says in our most important prayer, the Lord's Prayer, "... and forgive us our trespasses, as we forgive those who trespass against us."

> "This Taubmann was imprisoned for three-and-a-half months. Always staring death in the face. When they were taken to trial, he never knew if it was to the courts or to his execution. The man was freed a year ago – ludicrous! He is back in Afghanistan! Others would have to work through their trauma for two years. But he is back there and is doing something."
> Original recording of the former Employment and Social Policy Minister, Norbert Blum – Stern-TV

Georg and Marianne embrace after more than three months.

The three German women staff immediately after their release:

Margrit Stebner: I want to go back again – in spite of all the difficult experiences and dangers. What we experienced in prison has helped me to understand the Afghans better and to identify with their needs. We suffered in part with them and I want that to bring us closer together.

In addition, we now hope with some justification to be able to achieve more, above all with projects for women. I won't be discouraged and want to meet their needs as best I can.

Katrin Jelinek: Afghanistan is simply my place! They say, "Suffering creates close bonds!" I have got a deeper love for the country and the Afghans than I ever had before. I'm looking forward to the extension of the children's project in Kabul and especially that we can at last include the girls.

Afghanistan stands on the threshold of a new beginning and I want to be there. That is the task which God has given me and which gives meaning to my life.

Silke Dürrkopf: My job as a teacher of the children of the development staff was merely interrupted during the imprisonment. I feel committed to them. When the families fly back to Afghanistan, I'll be with them.

The street children and the construction of schools are also close to my heart. A few weeks ago I happened to see three of our street children in a picture of a crowd of people in Kabul in the *Frankfurter Allgemeine Zeitung*. They were wearing shoes and jackets which they had received from us last winter. When I saw them in the picture, I had a renewed sense that I belong in Afghanistan.

In April 2002, Georg Taubmann returned with his family—first to Pakistan and then, in June 2002, to Afghanistan. Silke Dürrkopf accompanied them and worked again for Shelter Now. She stayed till 2004. In October 2002 Margrit Stebner followed the Taubmann family. She remained till 2007. Katrin Jelinek returned to Kabul in 2007—together with her husband and two children. However one year later they had to return to Germany for health reasons.

In the Spotlight in Germany

Being imprisoned for more than three months inevitably leaves an impact. Even though Georg himself was not beaten, he was unable to purge his memory of the despairing cries of his fellow prisoners who had been abused. There was also the vivid memory of the filth, the insects, the cramped cell, and the dirty, stinking and overflowing toilets. There was the meager food, the lack of medical care, the isolation and the long trials. And the ever-present fear for his wife, Marianne, and his two sons. Above all the feeling of being totally at the mercy of these unpredictable, brutal men had embedded itself deep in his psyche.

And then, suddenly, the loud, garish, hectic life of freedom. There were many interviews in Islamabad with media from all over the world. Yet these were but a prelude to what was awaiting them in Germany.

Georg Taubmann: On our return to Germany, we spent about a week as a whole team at a secret location in France—well protected from press and publicity—to recover from the stress. We were able to sleep, go for walks, pray together—simply relax. Under guided supervision we chatted a lot with one another and learned for the first time how each of us had experienced and processed the days in prison. In addition, the psychologists gave us good tips on how to process our experiences in the future.

After that Marianne and I were able to have a few days holiday, but then it all took off in Germany … one engagement after another.

The mayor of Braunschweig invited Margrit, Katrin and Silke to the City Hall and honored them publicly. In the Braunschweig *Christuszentrum*, a Praise and Thanksgiving Service was held, in which hundreds of guests from home and abroad participated. And, of course, the press.

It was the same in Würzburg, Nürnberg, Munich and Berlin. Georg's home city of Sulzbach-Rosenberg gave a large reception. The four were ferried from place to place and had to tell their story again and again.

The three German Shelter Now colleagues (Margrit, Katrin and Silke) at the reception given by the mayor of their hometown, Braunschweig

REVIEW OF THE YEAR WITH GÜNTHER JAUCH

One of the highlights was taking part in the *Review of the Year* with the TV personality Günther Jauch. At the end of each year, Jauch presents an annual review of "People, Pictures, Emotions" on the TV station RTL. Jauch interviews prominent figures and personalities considered worthy of note in the past year. The year 2001 had, according to most assessments, been the most dramatic for decades. The whole world had been witness to the deadly and appalling attacks on the World Trade Center in New York on September 11. Because of that, the program featured some of those affected by the attack—including one of the courageous firefighters and some who had escaped.

But for Günther Jauch, the Shelter Now people were the highlight of the evening. Throughout the program their appearance to come was mentioned, until finally they appeared during the prime slot at program's end. Jauch already knew the Shelter Now volunteers from a previous broadcast in which he had interviewed Katrin's brother and the Chairman of Shelter Now Germany, Udo Stolte, while the hostages were still imprisoned. He had shown great sympathy towards them then. Now he was thrilled and delighted to see them alive and free right in front of him. Jauch's interview and comments were kind, sympathetic and glowing. And the nation watched.

Reception for the Foreign Office Crisis Committee

On the evening following the *Review of the Year* with Günther Jauch in Cologne, the Shelter Now team flew to Berlin to arrange a reception for the Foreign Office Crisis Committee.

The idea stemmed from Georg's brother. He called Udo Stolte, the Director of Shelter Now Germany. "Hey, the Crisis Committee got so involved on our behalf," he began. "They were always there for us. We must show our gratitude. Let's do something together. Money's no object. What if my brother were dead by now?

Can you not take that on?"

Udo called the Foreign Ministry. "Yes, we have something like a café upstairs. You could do something there," they said. "We also know a good catering service."

Udo Stolte: We had the space, now I had to get a guest list together. I invited everyone from the top: the Federal Chancellor, the Foreign Minister, the President. After all, the President of the USA, George W. Bush, had received the two freed Americans and shaken their hands. Everyone wrote back politely refusing. That left the Crisis Committee, some employees from the Foreign Ministry and from the Secret Service. I also invited the Diocesan Bishop from Wolfenbüttel, Christian Krause, to give a short devotional as he had done so much for us.

Georg Taubmann at the Annual Reception in Schloss Bellevue with President Johannes Rau

Together with our colleagues there were around 50 people. It was a lovely evening. At the conclusion the Head of the Crisis Committee said, "We have never experienced anything like this. We have been very involved with many citizens in crisis situations and rarely heard a word of thanks afterwards, but instead reproach. I consider it a great honor to have had a reception with so much gratitude from you."

RECEPTION BY THE FEDERAL PRESIDENT IN SCHLOSS BELLEVUE

Georg Taubmann: On January 6, 2002, a few weeks after the *Review of the Year* with Günther Jauch and the Crisis Committee Reception, we were invited to the Annual Presidential Reception with Federal President Johannes Rau and his wife in Schloss Bellevue. This was an even more important event, as on this occasion German citizens who have achieved something special are honored.

After our arrival in Berlin we were accommodated in a posh hotel. The following morning we were picked up and the red carpet was rolled out for us. The press surrounded us and carefully listened to every word the President spoke. On this occasion the President makes a formal declaration as to why the citizen concerned is being honored. He had only words of praise for our longstanding development aid projects in Pakistan and Afghanistan, above all for our "bravery and powers of endurance during our imprisonment."

After that, all of the coverage of Shelter Now in German newspapers and magazines featured only positive reporting. Georg was naturally delighted, since the very first press reports—some of which had reached them in prison—had

> **The Annual Presidential Reception**
>
> In order to participate in the Annual Presidential Reception at the Schloss Bellevue, the citizen must be proposed by an appropriate organization. The person and his involvement are then inspected by a State Commission, to see whether they merit such an honor. The Shelter Now projects were thoroughly assessed by the chief officer of the working panel Humanitarian Aid Abroad. On his return, he called Udo and had only very positive comments. "Mr. Stolte," he said, "I congratulate you on your work."
>
> At a meeting in Berlin of NGOs working in Afghanistan, he announced publicly: "The way Shelter Now works is the way humanitarian aid should be administered." During the imprisonment of the aid workers, Shelter Now's development projects in Pakistan had been visited by journalists from all over the world and examined closely – only the projects in Afghanistan were destroyed or closed. Pakistani and Afghan colleagues kept the projects in Pakistan going without any Western leadership. This autonomy made a deep impression on the journalists. The Afghan workers later told Georg that during his absence they were bombarded with questions, like whether they had been pressured—or even bribed—to convert religions.
>
> Of course, they firmly and credibly denied this.

been thoroughly accusatory and negative. As if they had behaved stupidly and irresponsibly got themselves in danger. The Taliban released false accusations that were uncritically accepted, portraying Shelter Now as spreading Christian material widely and using their relief aid and offers of education to convert Muslims. It would have required only a little research to reveal how groundless these accusations were. It was gratifying that this had been publicly corrected.

PRESS SCRUMS AND CRISIS MANAGEMENT IN GERMANY

Udo Stolte, the Director of Shelter Now Germany, was spending some time with his wife in Kabul when the two American women were apprehended by the Religious Police. On that fateful Friday evening, August 3, 2001, he took part in the volunteers' meeting and led the devotions. "During the course of the evening we became more and more anxious because the two women didn't turn up," he remembers. "Later we learned that they had been taken captive by the Taliban, but imagined that they would be released again after a few days … at worst expelled from the country."

The return flight was planned for Saturday, but the flight from Kabul was canceled. Thus Udo took a taxi on the Sunday morning and travelled the 280 km by road to the Shelter Now staff in Peshawar, Pakistan. From there he was supposed to fly back to Frankfurt via Dubai on Tuesday. Udo was under pressure as his school started on Wednesday.

Udo Stolte: It was in Peshawar that we learned through Radio Shariat that 24 Shelter Now colleagues had been taken captive, and charged with Christian proselytizing. My friend Georg was one of them. I was appalled! The top man in Shelter Now was in prison, and as number two in the leadership, I suddenly bore the whole burden of crisis management!

On Sunday evening I called a crisis meeting and gathered the Peshawar team around me. Everyone was totally shocked. White as sheets they crouched down in a circle, paralyzed. I had to get a grip on the situation. Fortunately I always had the ability to keep a cool head in a crisis. When, for example, an accident happened on a school outing and my colleagues reacted in total panic, I was able to think clearly and make the necessary decisions. It was the same now: *Who will deal with media questions? Who will inform the prayer partners? Who will be responsible for this and that?* I organized the staff and a semblance of peace returned to the group.

I took part in the prayers—for me it was 3 o'clock in the morning. While we were praying, I had the impression that God was speaking to me. *Udo, the press will descend on you like a flood. Have courage and jump into the flood. I am with you!* Up till then I had had little contact with the press. Writing an article here, an announcement there, that was all. I had no experience and no skills in dealing with the media. As would soon become clear, they were indeed very aggressive initially and knew how to ask combative questions.

The Shelter Now workers were taken captive at the weekend, Udo arrived in Braunschweig on the following Wednesday evening. He gave his colleagues in Braunschweig strict instructions to give no interviews as they had insufficient information at their disposal. But for the media the period from Sunday to Wednesday is a short eternity. As they got no information, they indulged in wild speculation.

Udo Stolte: At Braunschweig station, my colleagues met me straight away on the platform. Their first words were, "You've got to appear before the press. The reporters are on our heels and pressuring us continually for information."

But I was totally exhausted, sweaty and unshaven. "I can't appear before the press like this," I protested.

"But you must. They won't wait any longer." Scarcely had I arrived at the office and they were there—ARD, ZDF, the Braunschweig News and other journalists. The crazy thing was that they didn't want a general

---

Udo and Sieglinde Stolte have known and accompanied the Shelter Now organization since its inception. Udo has had a close relationship with Georg since the time Georg was living in Braunschweig. They were the contact persons in Germany for the Taubmanns and maintained a small home office from which they sent out information letters and managed donations.

In 1992, Udo visited Georg in Pakistan. "I returned from there a changed person," Udo asserts. "Never in my life have I witnessed such need and such misery. In the massive refugee camps I saw children playing in the sewer as if it were clean water. ... That turned my life upside down."

Back in Germany, Udo became more keenly involved in the aid projects. In 1993, Shelter Now Germany was founded. Udo was a primary school teacher. Soon he was no longer able to fulfill all his school commitments. Since 1996 he had been constantly reducing his hours—until, at the beginning of 2002, he gave up his teaching job altogether. From then on, he has officially headed up the German branch of Shelter Now International from Braunschweig.

press conference, but wanted to interview me personally, one after the other.

The next morning things really took off. At 6 o'clock, the first radio stations called and wanted to interview me on the phone for their early news bulletins. And so it continued, right through till the beginning of school. During my classes I didn't dare turn off my mobile phone. Each time it vibrated I glanced at the caller display. I knew that Georg had my number in his head, and I was clinging to the hope that he would contact me. Maybe he'd been released or could call me from the prison.

During the breaks between classes I dealt with the most urgent enquiries and after school I was straight back into the office. Different TV teams who again wanted to interview me personally were already awaiting me there. The whole afternoon went by in half-hour slots. While one broadcaster was dismantling his equipment and the next one setting his up, I was handling telephone interviews in between. That went on until early evening. Then I had a little peace, as the interviews had to be worked on by the journalists for the evening news. Later in the evening the enquiries came mostly from abroad.

The whole of the next few weeks followed the same pattern. But it wasn't only the press hustle and bustle, the whole crisis management fell on my shoulders. Relatives had to be kept informed and comforted, and churches who wanted to pray and to help needed to be updated. In addition I was constantly in touch with the Crisis Committee of the Foreign Office and with various Embassies.

Udo Stolte during a TV interview

During the three and a half months of the Shelter Now captivity as hostages, Udo estimates that he gave roughly around 1,000 interviews. Then when his friends were finally released, the inquiries increased dramatically. All the broadcasters descended on Udo, wanting to hear the very latest news. But it wasn't only in Germany that the media went wild. In Pakistan, too, 3,000 journalists from all over the world were waiting—so great was the interest in the hostage taking and the liberation of the eight Shelter Now workers.

On the night of their release Udo was just getting ready for a program with Günther Jauch.

Udo Stolte: With programs like that they keep the most exciting people till the end, so that the audience keeps watching and also sees lots of advertisements. I was sitting in the green room with the person who had prepared everything and taken the pre-interviews. There were snacks and I was following the program, when suddenly my mobile rang. Georg's brother Reinhold was at the other end. "Udo, something's going on. I just got a phone call that the Delta Force of the US Army is on its way." What that meant exactly we couldn't explain. But there was something in the air.

The person in charge noticed of course that something special was going on and asked inquisitively, "So, anything significant?" I put him off. I didn't want to share the news yet. I couldn't be sure. Shortly after the phone call came my part in the interview with Günther Jauch. I couldn't concentrate properly, because the thought was going round and round in my head *What if their release is happening right now?*

The broadcast was soon over and we were sitting together comfortably in the canteen. Günter Jauch sat down beside me at the table and was interested in knowing further details about my friends in Kabul. Previously the professional, now he was the private Günther Jauch.

During the conversation the phone rings again. This time it is the BBC. "Mr Stolte, we have heard something. What's going on there? Can you give us an interview?"

My answer: "I don't know anything definite. I cannot tell you anything." When further broadcasters call with the same question, I become suspicious and ring the Foreign Office.

"We know nothing," is their response.

"Then please get yourself some information, and call me back," I reply.

Then the evening is over, we're just arriving at the entrance to the hotel in a taxi. It is 2 o'clock in the morning. My mobile rings. It is the Foreign Office: "Mr. Stolte, we have good news for you. Your people are en route to Pakistan." Moved and beaming with joy, I relate this to the TV crew. And yes, I am besieged till 5 o'clock in the morning.

It has come this far. Excitedly Udo waits at Frankfurt Airport to be one of the first to greet his friends. A top official from the Foreign Office is there too. Udo had found out that there would be a press conference. "Can you please be there and support me?" Udo asks the official. The official agrees.

Udo Stolte: The journalists are already falling all over me. "Now that your colleagues are free, the two American women have admitted that they did proselytize using the Jesus film." Again the same old story.

"What did they do?" I reply. "They showed an excerpt from the Jesus film which can be bought in most Islamic countries. What's the problem?" That silenced the hecklers.

Then comes the next set of questions: "Your people said that they're going back." The implication being, that they want to put themselves in danger again and get themselves released at government expense.

"Yes, they said they would go back when the security situation allows it," I answer calmly.

"And what does the government have to say about that?" a journalist explodes. At this question all eyes turn to the government representative.

His inspired answer: "Throughout all the years Shelter Now has carried out fantastic work. There is scarcely any other organization which has brought so much change in Afghanistan. The Federal Government would be happy for these aid measures to continue."

It was good that the camera was focused on the Foreign Office official. At that moment, I probably looked like a rabbit caught in the headlights. The answer was simply brilliant.

Looking Back: Taken Hostage, Rescued

On every occasion that Georg talked about their arrest, the three-month captivity and their sudden release out of the hands of the Taliban—whether on Review of the Year with Günther Jauch or at the many celebratory church services and award ceremonies—the story of their dramatic release by American Special Forces is the most thrilling. Georg is a great storyteller! Listeners hang on his every word. Wild applause always follows. Many are amazed at the prudent, circumspect actions of the team leader and the good fortune they had. Others realize that God kept His protective hand over them. Georg himself is convinced: "If God had not worked so many miracles, we would probably not have come out alive."

The American Air Force is bombarding Kabul as a reaction to the attack on the World Trade Center in New York. The troops of the Northern Alliance are about to free the city—and also the eight Shelter Now workers—from Taliban rule. But heavily armed Taliban storm the prison. They intend to drag the Shelter Now volunteers off to Kandahar, the stronghold of Osama bin Laden and his Al Qaeda militia, as hostages. Kandahar is also the residence of Taliban leader Mullah Mohammed Omar. There goal was clearly to murder them there.

At an intermediate stop in Ghazni, a city under the control of the Taliban, the foreigners are housed in the city jail. Suddenly fighting between the local tribal people and the Taliban occupying forces breaks out. The insurgents storm the prison. Their strength is so superior that the Taliban have to flee without being able to take their hostages with them. All the prisoners are released, among them the eight Shelter Now development workers. Now, at last, the American Special Forces can be contacted and the liberation initiated. That, however, all proceeds more dramatically than planned.

TAKEN HOSTAGE

Excerpt from the book *Escape from Kabul*

Day 102: November 12, 2001

Georg Taubmann: "Mr. George," as I was called by the other Afghans imprisoned with me, "have you heard any news? How close is the Northern Alliance to Kabul now? Ten kilometres or less?"

Our fellow Afghan prisoners excitedly discussed the different possibilities. There were about 10 of them who had already received the death penalty. Some awaited amputation as punishment—they would have been the first to be killed by the guards in the event of a capitulation. And in spite of that they were deeply concerned about our uncertain fate—about my colleague Peter who shared a cell with me, as well as the six women who were held on the floor above us.

The sound of airplanes penetrated the prison walls. Heavy artillery fire could be heard coming closer and closer and considerably more frequently than it had been in recent days. The walls shook, window panes rattled, the floor vibrated and the tension was almost unbearable. The Afghan prisoners were running excitedly to and fro in the corridor between the cells.

As 8 o'clock approached, I became really restless; with the best will in the world I could not see any way out of our increasingly dangerous situation. On the one hand, possible bombing of the prison; on the other, brainless Taliban fighters who could do whatever they wanted with us. What was I to do? The confusion and the tension were tearing me apart to such an extent that I could hardly think straight. And I was the one supposed to be making the right decisions at this crucial moment. Fear gripped me. What if some harm should come to one of the eight of us right before being released? I didn't dare think about it.

"If the Taliban dare to touch you foreigners, we will defend you," said Mustafa, who had touchingly cared for us in recent weeks and had become my friend. He kept making plans as to how he could free us from the dreadful prison. One time he had even acquired special saw-blades from the bazaar and got them smuggled into our wing of the prison.

"Here, I've got something for you. We can saw through the bars and get you out."

"Thank you that you are so concerned about us, Mustafa. But I can't agree. I don't want anyone to be put in danger or indeed shot dead while trying to escape," I responded.

Now he took me aside again and pleaded with me. "You know, we're sure the Taliban are coming and they'll abduct you. Who knows what they'll do to you? They'll kill you or drag you off to Kandahar."

"But what can we do about it?" I asked in despair.

"Listen! We have a plan. I've spoken to some of the guards upstairs and paid them off. They won't stand in our way. But they know that the game's up. We've hidden three Kalashnikovs (sub-machine guns designed in Russia) in a small room. At 11 o'clock we'll go upstairs and spend the night there. When the Taliban come we'll overpower them and make off in their vehicles."

Oh no, I thought, *there's no way this can end well!*

But despite many persuasive arguments I could not deter my friend from his plan. So I kept quiet.

The ceiling above me was shaking from the heavy artillery fire, although our wing of the prison was almost two meters under ground. The pressure and the sense of panic broke me out in a cold sweat. In order to find some sort of peace, I crawled into a tiny box-room and groaned, "Oh, God! Don't allow them to kill us or to take us captive—and please not to Kandahar!" Slowly I became calmer.

Outside in the prison yard there was a sudden commotion. I could hear rough commands being shouted. Vehicles came and went. Presumably valuable objects and important documents were being removed.

There's something brewing! I've got to speak to our women colleagues. But how? My brain was spinning. I went to the guards and said, "I've got to go up to the women and fetch some medication. Diana is a nurse."

One of them led me upstairs. I knocked on their cell door and quickly gave the women my instructions: "The Northern Alliance is only a few kilometers from Kabul. Something's going to happen in the next few hours and it may be dramatic." I tried hard not to show my anxiety.

"Barricade the cell door. Whatever happens, don't open it until you hear me. We must do everything possible to stick together!"

I spoke in German so that the guard couldn't understand. Then I took the packet of medicines and ambled as casually as possible back downstairs.

Georg had been able to warn the women just in the nick of time. Shortly before 10 o'clock, some vehicles suddenly showed up. Footsteps echoed through the entrance. Keys jangled at the main gate. A noisy group of Taliban ran down the corridors and hammered on the door of the cell where the six women were being held. "Open up! Open up! Out, out!"

"No," answered Diana firmly. "We'll only come out when Georg comes." The men, furious, kept hammering on the door.

"Get Georg and Peter here and we'll open up!"

Diana knew only too well that it would have been no problem for the Taliban to knock down the door, but she remained firm. The men surprisingly gave in to her refusal and stormed down to Peter and Georg's cell below.

In the meantime Georg and Peter both heard the excited voices of the men above them. They were incredibly fearful about their female colleagues. Then they found themselves staring at tense Taliban with the safety catches of their Kalashnikovs released. Hurriedly, they packed a few of their belongings and rushed upstairs.

When they reached the women's cell, Georg shouted nervously, "Diana,

Diana, open up! They are really serious. They'll shoot!"

The women quickly opened the door.

"Get out!" the guards ordered. "You don't need to take anything with you. We're only taking you to a safe location for the night."

But the women took no notice. They had been lied to too many times. So they quickly packed their blankets and their few pieces of clothing. Then the eight of them were shoved outside where two vehicles stood waiting. The Taliban intended to separate them into two groups.

Whatever happens, we must stay together! was Georg's constant thought.

In the previous weeks, he had constantly been worried that something could happen to the women if they fell into the hands of vengeful Taliban, without the men.

So Georg insisted, "We are not going to be separated."

As time was pressing, the guards agreed. With their pitiful luggage, they stumbled on to the two benches in the back of the Toyota Land Cruiser. An armed guard crouched beside them. It was only then that Georg noticed several live grenades lying on the floor. When the vehicle finally raced away, they were jumbled together in a heap. The second vehicle, packed with more armed Taliban, followed them.

Margrit Stebner: It was quite a shock for me when they took us out of the cell. Suddenly these aggressive men with their Kalashnikovs at the ready! You could see that they wouldn't show much consideration. You don't forget that sight. Hours previously I'd felt intuitively that something awful was going to happen to us. I was quite churned up inside.

I was the first one to climb into the Land Cruiser and I landed in a corner at the front on the Taliban's baggage. Then our luggage was added, leaving me half buried under it all. I could hardly move, I could barely breathe and I was having real panic attacks. And then I realized we were going in the direction of Kandahar, even though Georg evaded our questions. The whole business was so surreal, so uncanny. So all I could do was pray. I had no words. I just suppressed the fear deep inside. At the same time I had an unforgettable experience in the midst of the chaos. It was as if someone inside me was laughing. An inner voice said, *You're on the way to freedom!*

That can't be true, I thought. And yet, I felt God very close. The sense of oppression and panic had gone.

Georg Taubmann: *Where might they be taking us?* I thought. *To another prison or maybe to Kandahar?*

First we traveled to the city center. I knew the area well. The driver raced along the streets so fast that we almost had an accident. They were in a huge hurry!

We passed the Hotel Intercontinental, then down the street to a large silo. I thought: *Now we're going to the road that leads to Wardak, from there to Ghazni and then on to Kandahar.*

The women were anxious, but kept remarkably calm.

"Georg, do you know where we are?" one of them asked. "Where are we heading to?"

I simply didn't want to mention the name of this terrifying city so I replied, "I think we're heading to Wardak."

"And where is Wardak? Is that towards the Pakistani border?" "No, not exactly."

Then we were out of the city and clearly going in the direction of Kandahar. The arterial road was crammed with vehicles with fleeing Taliban fighters. But our two jeeps careened past the string of cars at breakneck speed. Armed men crowded every road. It was unbelievable how many people were fleeing from the city as fast as they could. I caught sight of some army tanks traveling south. The incessant bombing had so worn down the fighters that they were taking to their heels in panic.

We overtook them all and sped past them. After about an hour we turned off the road and onto a track that led us to a village. Here we were greeted by Mullah Hassan Yashim. He was a top official in the Taliban regime and responsible for our imprisonment.

Aha, I thought to myself, *it was too hot for you in Kabul so you got out before us.*

Mullah Hassan Yashim got into the second jeep. I felt very uneasy—indeed I was seized with fear. This man was capable of anything. That he had personally received us was not a good sign. In the prison he was considered especially cruel, as he himself gratuitously beat and tortured prisoners. He hadn't beaten us, but he had always been rough and unfriendly.

Our journey continued for another two or three hours as we raced past darkened villages. Again and again we were stopped at checkpoints—roadblocks—where we were inspected. Each time I hoped that they'd recognize us as foreigners ... maybe even set us free.

Completely exhausted, disappointed and discouraged, I crouched down in the back of the Land Cruiser. Just a couple of hours before the liberation of Kabul we found ourselves hostages on the way to the most horrific place in Afghanistan! And we had dreamt of dancing on the streets of Kabul with the other prisoners, celebrating the end of Taliban rule.

Day 103: 13. November 2001

Georg Taubmann: About 1 o'clock in the morning the convoy turned off the main road into a village. Small mud houses hid behind high walls. *At last a break*, I thought. *We can spend the night in the houses.* I stretched my legs and prepared to get out.

But no! The jeep rocked across an open field to a rusty, battered steel container, the sort of container which is normally used to transport goods on the back of trucks to transatlantic cargo ships. We froze with shock when we saw it.

Panic stricken, some of us protested. "That's impossible! We're not going in there. We'll not survive!"

I tried to persuade the guards. "Please, take us into the houses! Don't do this to us! Have you no mercy?"

But they wouldn't relent. I bargained with them to at least leave the door open. Now they gave way, but we didn't trust them. So Heather sat down in the entrance to the container and, despite persuasion and threat, refused to move one centimeter into the container. Inside were some filthy mattresses and ragged blankets. At least we'd have some covering. This night was going to be cold.

The whole scene was completely surreal. At the door Heather engaged in debate with the armed guard so that she wouldn't fall asleep.

"Where can we go to the toilet?" enquired Margrit.

Without a word the guards pointed to the open field. What did it matter to them that the women had to relieve themselves under their curious gaze? It was simply inhuman.

For most of us the night was horrendous and sleep impossible. The temperature fell below zero. The women shivered and moved closer to each other to try and get warm. Peter and I shared one blanket. We all awaited the dawn full of dark premonition.

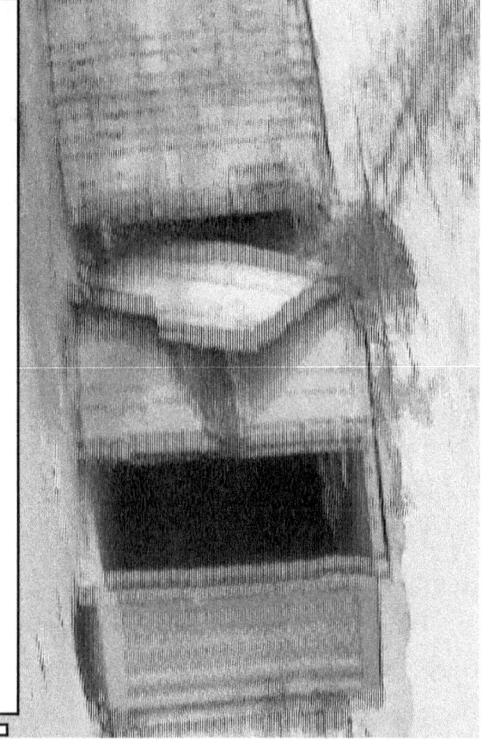

> When driving through the outer suburbs of Kabul, one cannot fail to notice the battered, crumpled steel containers partly riddled with bullets. After the Soviet withdrawal, the mujahideen, during their usurpation of power, often drove opponents and civilians into these containers. One of them would throw a live hand grenade inside and slam the door. This metallic evidence of dreadful murders is shattering to every passerby who experienced the horror of this period. And some of the Shelter Now staff knew of this savagely brutal Taliban practice.

A shipping container often used during the civil wars as a prison or place of execution

Margrit Stebner: When I had to enter the container, I was panic stricken. *They'll lock us in and blow us up with a hand grenade!* In order somehow to keep myself calm, at first I stood at the edge of all that was going on and observed the chaos. Heather was debating with some men, Georg, wildly gesticulating, was bargaining with the others. Again I felt panic rising within me. This mixture of helplessness, anger and fear of death is a terrible thing. In spite of everything, within me I heard, as I had earlier in the jeep, the calming words, *Margrit, it is okay. You are on the way to freedom!* When I heard that, I was able to lie down in peace beside the other women.

Georg Taubmann: At 6 o'clock the mullah arrived. He had obviously found a more comfortable place than ours to spend the night in the village. Not a drop of tea, not a morsel of food for us. Instead we were again stuffed into the back of the jeep and off we went. Now Mullah Hassan Yashim himself drove us. *We must be a very valuable bargaining chip for him,* I thought.

"Mullah Hassan, what's going on?" I asked the big chief. "Where are you taking us?"

"To Ghazni!" came the brusque reply. "We're taking you to a warm house. You can get warm there, freshen up and have breakfast."

So Mullah Hassan Yashim intended to make a stop there. I knew that Ghazni was his hometown and his family lived there.

We were reassured on the one hand by the Mullah's words; on the other we knew we couldn't trust him. We drove into the city and straight towards an ugly building with high walls and barred windows. "Oh God, please, not another prison!" We were all petrified.

Fortunately we drove on by; we all breathed a sigh of relief. A stroke of luck! But no, he had only taken the wrong road. He turned around and headed straight into the dark prison entrance. What an emotional roller coaster!

"Mullah," I said, "you promised to take us to a proper house!"

"Get out! And make it quick!" was his response.

We were immediately surrounded by guards, their Kalashnikovs at the ready. Any resistance was pointless. We had no choice other than to enter this terrible building. Outside we could hear artillery fire.

They locked us into two attached rooms on the first floor. I could scarcely believe my eyes when I saw the toilet—a stinking, blocked up hole in the ground and all around it piles of human excrement. The worst we had ever seen. And we were to stay here?

Again we heard the sound of bombing, so severe that the whole building shook. At this, one of our women had a panic attack and ran out into the corridor, where she crouched at the door weeping.

"Get inside!" the guard screamed at her. "You can't stay here!"

In total desperation she pleaded with him, but he showed no mercy. So I tried to persuade him. "Let her sit there. Don't you see that she's terrified? We're not about to run away."

Fortunately I was able to change his mind. However, we were all having to combat panic. We had just escaped the bombing in Kabul and now the sound of battle in Ghazni, of all places! What was happening? The Northern Alliance with its troops was far away.

Slowly we got accustomed to our new environment. The women began to clear the place and laid mattresses on the floor. We squatted down on the floor and decided at least to eat breakfast. The guards actually brought us *naan*—bread—and green tea. One of us managed to unearth a small piece of cheese. Above all, we were pleased to be all together, unscathed.

Following breakfast we thanked God for all his protection and prayed for one another, especially for Margrit who had become very weak because of dysentery, and for me that I would be able to make the right decisions.

While we were still sitting there the shooting started up again, very loud and violent. Then we heard the uproar approaching the prison.

One of us ran to the window and described what could be seen. "They're fighting right in front of the prison. Is that the Taliban or not? Now lots of people are running away!"

Suddenly, it became deathly quiet. Not a single shot, not a sound could be heard.

It seemed to us like an eternity. But then there was a large crowd of people in front of the prison who were trying to break open the gates. One of us looked out of the window again and shouted, "There's a crowd of people, young people, too. They're coming in!"

Wild thoughts swirled through my head. *The mob will storm the prison and lynch us foreigners.* I was massively afraid. What I had always dreaded was to be abducted or lynched. I had observed lynch murders in Pakistan, and I would have much preferred to be shot!

On the ground floor the doors were smashed open. Then they were hammering on the door to our floor till it eventually broke open with a loud crash. Some men stormed towards our cells and ripped the doors open.

And so it happened that suddenly standing in front of us was a sweating Afghan, cartridge belt across his chest, Kalashnikov swinging to and fro. Totally flabbergasted at seeing foreigners in front of him, he paused. For some moments we stared at each other speechless, as if paralyzed.

I was wondering why he was looking so surprised. Didn't he know that we were there. Suddenly I thought, *Maybe he is not a Talib but somebody from the opposition.* I hardly dared to ask and, deeply scared, I asked him in Pashtu: "Who are you? Are you from the opposition?

He then answered, "Yes."

I hardly could believe it and asked him again, "Are you from Massood's party?" He again said, "Yes, yes, we are Massood's people!"

This was an unbelievable moment. Beside myself with happiness and relief, I embraced him. Some of the women began to weep. Seconds earlier we had hoped that they wouldn't find us, or if they did, that they would kill us mercifully. And the next, moment we were free.

More and more men pushed their way into our cell. (Ahmed Shah Massood was a highly respected military leader of the Northern Alliance, who had been assassinated on September ninth.)

"Now you must get out. Quickly, quickly, now. Go. You are really free!"

We didn't need to be told twice; we rushed outside. The atmosphere was bristling with tension. The shooting was still going on and a rocket launcher had been set up in front of the prison.

"Quick, in here!"

In order to be shielded from the shooting we had to wait for a while in a small lookout post by the prison wall. Only then were we able to escape into freedom. We ran as fast as we could, totally unprotected, across an open space. Then the first buildings came into view where we were able to find shelter.

We crossed a sort of housing settlement. When the owners discovered us, they emerged from their houses and stared at us in amazement. But we were not alone. One of the fighters led us through the streets. We crisscrossed the streets until a commander appeared and led us to his office.

The farther we went, the larger grew the crowd of curious people who accompanied us. They were chatting loudly. "Who are these foreigners? Where do they come from?" No one had known anything about us. Then suddenly, the spell broke! Someone hugged us, numerous people shook our hands, slapping us on the shoulders. The crowd began to cheer. Men took our luggage from us and carried the women's bundles. It was simply indescribable.

Silke Dürrkopf: This march through the street of Ghazni was one of the most wonderful experiences of our whole imprisonment. I had written to my friends back home, "I long that one day I will dance with the Afghans on the streets of Kabul celebrating their liberation from the Taliban." As it hadn't happened there, this was a sort of compensation for me. It was simply wonderful! At that moment I wasn't at all concerned that we were still in danger. One of the Taliban could have removed his turban, mingled among the crowd and shot us dead. I was completely exhausted and yet happy. How thankful I was when a man took my awkward bundle of blankets from me! The atmosphere was like a folk festival!

Margrit Stebner: For me the whole liberation story was like an emotional roller coaster. My feelings peaked and plunged and in between stood on their head. One moment scared to death and then suddenly the giddiness of being set free.

In retrospect I am very grateful that it was Afghans who set us free. That brought me a certain healing: malicious Afghans had imprisoned us, loving Afghans liberated and cheered us.

RELEASED IN THE NICK OF TIME!
Excerpt from the book *Escape from Kabul*

Day 103: November 13, 2001

The eight Shelter Now aid workers were led by a group of fighters through the streets of Ghazni, accompanied by a steadily growing crowd of curious people, to a sort of office.

There they were greeted by a man who could speak a little English. "Welcome, I am Mohammed Salim, a security officer in this city," he introduced himself.

He was obviously the leader of the group who had rescued them from prison. Immediately tea was brought, and they were able to use the toilet, freshen up and catch their breath. The office was overflowing with people and more armed men kept arriving. Some were just curious about the foreigners, others were given commands and hurried away again.

The atmosphere was turbulent and tense. The citizens of Ghazni were probably completely surprised by the liberation of their city from the Taliban and were not quite sure just who should now take on leadership.

In the course of the afternoon a group of wild looking fighters stormed into the office; their leader insisted on speaking to the Shelter Now people, which Mohammed Salim did not permit. They argued loudly in Dari and spoke over the top of one another to such an extent that the eight foreigners could scarcely understand any of the conversation. Eventually the security officer sent this group away again.

Georg Taubmann, who was closely observing the situation and the atmosphere around him, realized right away that the various ethnic groups in the city were vying for power and that he and his colleagues obviously were in the keeping of Mohammed Salim. As the man gave the impression of being levelheaded and competent, that was fine with Georg.

At about 12 o'clock, lunch was finally brought into the office, Kabuli pulao, rice mixed with sultanas and meat, a real festive meal. They all enjoyed the substantial meal together, and chatted among themselves, allowed themselves to feel happy and enjoy the pleasure of their relief about their release. A great mood prevailed in the office.

Georg Taubmann: I imagined everything would now go smoothly. I assumed that we would find an office somewhere with a phone, call the German embassy in Pakistan from there and say, "Hello, we're free! Send a helicopter to Ghazni and pick us up!"

So I pressed our new host. "Where is there a telephone here? I've got to phone our embassy in Islamabad urgently and tell them that we are free."

"Just a minute, just a minute," Mohammed Salim answered. "We have two or three offices in the city which have satellite phones."

At last we got going, that is Mohammed Salim and I and a whole group of guards. The other seven of our team waited in the office.

On the streets lots of people were celebrating. You could sense joy at the liberation from the Taliban, but at the same time there was palpable tension in the air. Three different ethnic sections of the population lived together in Ghazni—Pashtuns, Tajiks and Hazaras—who were now drawing up their different power boundaries. Consequently, lots of armed men were running around.

Our path led us past looted shops. I saw that street barriers had already been erected, and there was occasional shooting. The mood was slowly turning into mistrust among the ethnic groups, presumably out of fear of revenge attacks. These fears were not unjustified, as the Pashtuns, many of whom belonged to the Taliban, had behaved brutally towards the Tajiks and the Hazaras in the past.

At last we reached the official telephone exchange, but it had been destroyed and plundered. So our search continued. The two businesses which were supposed to have satellite phones were shut, probably from fear of looting. We had to return to the office without having achieved anything. Mohammed Salim was clearly anxious and the guards at the street barriers eyed us suspiciously before they allowed us through.

After a short discussion, Mohammed Salim decided to accommodate the Shelter Now staff with a relative called Hamisha Gul, who owned a house outside of the city. In order to get there, they had to drive through a section of the city mostly populated by Hazaras. Again and again they encountered groups of men armed

The eight hostages after their release from the prison in Ghazni

with weapons and grenades. The driver maneuvered the minibus as quickly as possible through the streets. Everyone heaved a sigh of relief when they finally reached the property in the suburbs.

The owner must have been quite wealthy as his property consisted of several buildings surrounded by high walls. They were warmly received and the women were immediately shown a room where they could rest. It was roomy and furnished with mattresses and carpets. Finally they were able to shower and have some rest.

While the women were relaxing, Georg Taubmann sat with the Afghan men in a neighboring room, drinking tea. At last he could turn on the radio, which he had hidden in his waistcoat pocket, and listen to the news. He learned that Kabul had been taken by the troops of the Northern Alliance on the same night as they had been captured. People were celebrating and dancing on the streets of Kabul.

That grieved him because they would have gladly joined in. Then he thought again about how he could get to a telephone to contact the German Embassy in Islamabad. The situation in Ghazni was really frightening. Time was pressing.

Something had to be done.

For Georg, the break was only a short one. Soon he was heading back into the city escorted by guards. This time to the International Red Cross office, from where he hoped to be able to contact Islamabad.

Georg knew this building as he had spent the night in their guest rooms three years earlier on a trip to a Shelter Now project in Kandahar with three friends. He had made good contact with the staff. When they arrived, he was recognized at once. The Afghan Red Cross staff had been following the fate of the Shelter Now people the entire time and were happy to see them now unharmed and free.

They immediately offered Georg all possible help. They contacted the International Red Cross in Islamabad and enquired how they could get the eight foreigners safely out of the country.

Happy with this partial success Georg went back to his accommodation and waited. During the night, however, he could scarcely sleep a wink. Peter and he had to share a room with 10 to 15 men who constantly listened to the radio, smoked and conversed with one another.

The Afghans took turns guarding the house. Five of them patrolled alternately outside, constantly wary. They had every reason to be concerned that the Hazaras might take revenge on the owner and attack the house. After all, the owner had collaborated with the Taliban, which had terribly harassed this tribal group.

In the International Red Cross office in Islamabad

Day 104: November 14, 2001

Early Wednesday morning, they were off to the Red Cross office again. The staff had received a reply from Islamabad, but unfortunately the Red Cross were unable to provide a helicopter to fly them out. That would have been the quickest and safest way.

But the Red Cross was prepared to drive the aid workers to Kabul since the city had been freed. Then the eight could be flown out more easily from there. But there were still too many checkpoints controlled by the Taliban en route. At any of these, they would definitely be discovered and captured. The land route was therefore impossible. The only remaining possibility was to link up with the American forces and be flown out by them.

"But then it's a military action and has many associated risks," the Red Cross staff member warned. But for Georg, that was the least of his worries, and he agreed. The International Red Cross in Islamabad contacted the American Embassy and they commissioned one of their secret Afghan agents to travel from Kabul to Ghazni and give Georg a satellite phone. The journey from Ghazni to Kabul takes about five or six hours. The messenger was a Pashtun with a typical long beard. On the road to Ghazni he was taken for a Taliban and nearly arrested. But he was able to talk his way out of it and they let him go. He reached the Red Cross office and identified himself as a secret collaborator with the Americans.[2]

Of course, no one from the new protectors in Ghazni knew anything of this meeting. They were discussing how best to protect their guests and how they might be released. The danger was great that fighting could break out between the opposing ethnic groups in Ghazni. While the negotiations went on and on, a messenger arrived from their host and informed Georg that he and his colleagues absolutely had to move to another house.

"Out there in the outskirts of the city it's too dangerous," he reasoned. "We can't protect you well enough there, if we were to be attacked by the insurgent Hazaras. We have another house closer in to the city, but your team colleagues refuse to go without your agreement. Please write a letter to say you agree."

Georg Taubmann could well understand his people. All too often they had been moved with great and wordy promises and the situation had always become worse. No wonder doubts and fears arose. But he also understood the host's reasons and saw how the danger was intensifying. So he quickly wrote a note saying, "It's okay for you to move to the other house. I'm still here negotiating, will come as soon as possible to the new place. Things going well."

After a few more things had been clarified, Georg was taken to the new house by Mohammed Salim and his accomplices. These new quarters right on the edge of the city were rather smaller, but surrounded by a high wall, as is usual in Afghanistan. They had lunch together there and Georg informed his team how the negotiations had gone.

Suddenly the head of the Red Cross arrived and told Georg that he should come at once to the office. Someone wanted to see him there.

Georg Taubmann: That made me curious. Who on earth would want to speak to me so urgently? The commandant, a little suspicious, took me with his escort to the Red Cross office.

Under the pretext of having to go to the toilet, I was led into a side room and there sat an Afghan smiling at me. "How did you get here?" I was completely nonplussed— I recognized him from our time in the prison. He had often looked after us there and mediated between us and the Taliban guards. After his release, he had made contact with the Americans in order to help us. During the conversation, he secretly transferred a satellite telephone to me, into which the number for the Special Forces had been programmed. I only had to press it and at once I was connected with those in charge of the action. At last I was able to call them. I identified myself and described where we were, but first of all my opposite number wanted to speak to the two Americans. The head of the Red Cross set off immediately and brought them. Only after the two women had identified themselves did the action start rolling.

Together with the Red Cross colleagues, we arranged by phone where they could pick us up in the military helicopters. They didn't want to fly into the city. A spot outside Ghazni was arranged. The instruction was to drive there at twelve midnight and lay a flag on the ground. They would then fly over it and note the spot.

> The US forces were very well informed about the situation in Ghazni. The general situation was extremely uncertain and could change from one minute to the next. In trying to rescue the team, they could easily have been drawn into a civil war within the city. As it was a case of an unexpected local insurgency in Ghazni, the American Special Forces could not depend on the support of the Northern Alliance during this exercise. Their troops were very far away. Ghazni was like an island surrounded on every side by districts which were firmly under Taliban rule. Moreover, the Americans knew that Taliban fighters on the run were already preparing a counter-attack on the city. The situation was explosive and the time short. So they pressed Georg Taubmann to keep to their prearranged time.

At exactly that time we were to sit down in a row on the ground.

In the meantime the commander had left again. When he returned, I informed him delightedly that the American Special Forces would pick us up in their helicopters the next morning at a certain place outside Ghazni. Although everything seemed to now be clear, suddenly one problem after another emerged. Some wanted to chat first to the new dictators in Ghazni about our rescue by the American Special Forces. Still others were against that, especially the commander. "No, that's too dangerous! There could be secret followers of the Taliban among the new dictators who will hand our foreign friends over to them if they can."

Then one of the most important men refused to drive us to the agreed meeting point. "The place is too far outside the city. There's a curfew and it's far too dangerous to drive through the city at this hour."

Now there was no one prepared to take us to the appointed place. The nocturnal rescue mission was too dangerous for them. They were also clearly afraid of having problems with the new city rulers.

Irritated and disappointed, I called the Americans. "Guys, it's not working out! The Afghans here won't cooperate. It's just too dangerous for them. You'll have to get us during the day."

"No way!" was the decisive response of the American military. "You've got to be brought out tonight and at the appointed time!"

As the roadblocks had already been set up, the Afghans were pushing to leave for their night quarters. On leaving, the Red Cross staff member managed to pass the satellite phone secretly to Georg. Gratefully he hid the device in his *salwar kameez*[3] and held his hand protectively over it. The streets were completely empty except for the posts at the road barriers. Georg Taubmann's watchers drove him home, their primed Kalashnikovs at the ready. And when a pickup truck with armed men approached them, both his guards and the men in the other vehicle aimed their guns at one another. Cold sweat ran down Georg's back. The fighters eyed each other with animosity and drove on.

When Georg arrived at his accommodation, his colleagues were awaiting him anxiously. They hadn't seen him the whole afternoon and had been worrying whether everything would go as planned.

Totally depressed Georg squatted down beside his people and began to report: "The Americans want to pick us up at any cost in a few hours quite near here.

But our Afghan hosts and their commandant are refusing to let us out of the house at night. I don't know how we're to get out of this house with these high walls and being under strict guard. You must pray! I'm going to try and persuade the men here in the house to change their minds."

Georg argued with the guards, at his wits' end. "Please let us out! Open the gate! Our freedom is so close! Have you no mercy?"

"No, we're not opening the gate. We're not letting you out. Only the commander can give the order and he's not here."

"Then send him a message or bring him here!"

"That's not on. There's a curfew. We cannot leave the house."

And so it went on, back and forth. The men were not to be persuaded. Their fear of acting against the commander's orders was too great.

Georg Taubmann: When the guards lay down to sleep, I slipped out into the inner courtyard and contacted the Americans again. Their first questions were, "Where have you been the whole time? Where are you now?" They wanted to know our exact location. Then they said, "Do a GPS reading. Send us your GPS coordinates." I didn't know how to do that, so they directed me through the menu. I promised to do the GPS reading right away and to contact them with the information. I quickly fetched Peter who wrote down all the data. Then I called back and gave them the coordinates. It's unimaginable what would have happened if our guards had caught me doing this. The Americans praised me highly. "Super, we know now exactly where you are. Come at midnight to the prearranged spot."

They described the route. "Out through the gate, then right and then after 100 meters, left, etc."

"Yes, but we can't get out of here," I replied. "The people are armed; there's a high wall."

Their answer: "Then you'll have to kill the two guards." He offered to give me a crash course over the phone on how to kill them without using weapons.

"I won't do that. I'm killing no one," I groaned.

"Yeah, you must do it," he insisted. "If you don't do it, then we'll come and do it." After that we broke off our conversation because I wasn't having any of it. We had always prayed that if we were released no one should die, and now this.

After this I didn't know what I should do next. I was incredibly tense. *Now the Special Forces are coming to this house in order to set us free, and there will definitely be deaths*, was my only thought. Desperately I prayed and then got an idea. I wakened the guards and showed them the satellite phone. "Listen, you people, let us go. I have informed the Americans. They know exactly where we are. They're already on the way here in their helicopters." They blew their top in panic; it was total chaos. Their shouting wakened everyone in the house. The Afghan women wept in despair. Then they forced me to call the Americans back and tell them they were not to come. "That doesn't concern us" was their straight answer, "they are to let you go, then nothing will happen to them."

A short time later the sounds of a military aircraft could be heard circling over the city. Now the Afghans were more and more terrified. And still they didn't dare to open the gate and let the Shelter Now people out.

Their fear of the commander was too great.

Georg went across to the women and groaned, "Everything's getting more and more crazy. They simply won't allow us out of the house."

"Oh God, help us," they prayed together. "We are so close to being set free. Do a miracle, so that they will let us go."

In the meantime, it was already half past eleven. It was dreadful to see time slipping away. The tension became unbearable. On the one hand the desperate house owners were pressuring Georg and on the other their rescue was so near. Georg felt his head would explode. Meanwhile the helicopter sounds of their liberators could be heard clearly above the city—and it was as if they were behind cage bars. It was intolerable!

Then suddenly a vehicle drove up and there was loud knocking on the barricaded gate. Everyone was shocked and startled. Who might be coming at this hour during curfew? Helper or enemy?

Some of the guards went anxiously downstairs. A little later Georg heard them negotiating at the gate, then he saw the commander coming up the steps. Where did he come from so quickly?

Thank you, Lord! thought Georg.

From his home the commander had heard first the sounds of the aircraft and then the helicopter and was able to work out that the American liberators were approaching, despite his refusal to let the aid workers go. For this reason he intended to move the eight as quickly as possible to another location.

"You must leave this house immediately," he shouted at them. "The Taliban who dragged you here to Ghazni have come back. They know where you are and want to kill you. Get your things quickly. I'll take you to a safer place."

Georg Taubmann: I was totally shocked, as if paralyzed. *That can't be true. Are those people after us already? Now, just before our rescue! Is this terror never going to end?* These were the thoughts spinning around in my head.

The next moment I knew without a doubt, *What the commander is saying isn't true! It's only a trick!* The commander knew how much we feared our kidnappers and he just wanted to stop us from meeting up with the American rescuers.

Outwardly calm I went up to the man, stood in front of him and said, "We are not coming with you. We've had enough. Why are you not letting us go? Don't you hear the helicopters on the way? We are not moving from this spot, otherwise you can shoot us!"

In Kabul I'd never have dared to say anything like that; the cruel men there would have shot us right away. But now I took a chance. Somehow these people here were more human. Uncertain, he turned his back on me and discussed furiously with his men. I just stood there, prayed quietly and waited. Then he came up again to me and ordered me to follow him. Again, I calmly gave him the same answer. "We are not coming with you. Then you'll have to shoot us!" My stubbornness seemed to confuse him.

In that moment we could hear the sound of the helicopter far in the distance but clearly. The commander heard it and suddenly turned around and went back to his people and they left.

The timing was perfect, to the minute. If the commandant had had even 10 more minutes, he could have knocked me down and removed us all by force. But the helicopters were roaring so menacingly that he panicked, ran to his car and drove away.

We ran along the mud road in complete darkness. One of the house owners accompanied us. Along right then left again and yes, there is the place they described! I took out the satellite phone and yelled into it, "We're here!"

"Fantastic, George. Just sit down. Relax!"

"Shall I do another coordinate reading?" I asked.

"No, not necessary." … and bang! The telephone was dead. Battery dead. No more connectivity to the rescuers.

Margrit Stebner: We had spent the whole afternoon in a state of tension. Our mood kept swinging from hope to fear. It was also quite late when Georg returned. We could see that he was completely past it.

"It's probably not going to work out tonight," he said, utterly depressed, as he explained the muddled situation to us. When he went again to the watchmen in the courtyard to try to persuade them, we began to pray again.

The Afghan women who were sitting with us were afraid that something awful would happen to them during the American rescue mission. When there was a knock on the door they panicked. They pulled us into the house, wept and shook with fear. We too were close to desperation.

I could hear Georg arguing with someone in the courtyard. Then suddenly we heard him shouting, "It's worked! Right, get out! Quick, leave everything behind! Run!" Then we ran. It was completely dark and the path was rough. I fell into a pothole but Katrin grabbed me by the hand and we ran on. It wasn't far; it took only about 20 minutes for us to reach the place.

Day 105: November 15, 2001

A while before the agreed time, the eight aid workers sat in a row on the ice-cold ground, as had been earlier arranged, and heard the helicopters approaching. In their haste, they had been able to bring only a small lamp as a signal, which gave out too little light to be seen from a height. Moreover, it didn't correspond to the agreement made with the American Special Forces.

Everywhere in the city, small fires flickered. How were the rescuers to distinguish their lamp from the other lights? The inhabitants had lit these fires because they were cold, as they had remained up and were keeping watch outside, out of concern that the Taliban militia might return.

Then, suddenly, a huge helicopter rumbled past very low and close to them.

"Did he see us? Surely he spotted us! Here we are!" the eight shouted over the noise while waving madly. But the machine pulled away and flew off in the direction of another sector of the city. The Shelter people were horrified. "Have the Americans given up? Are they flying away?"

Then the helicopter came back and flew past them very close. In doing so it made a dreadful noise. The people in front of their houses were becoming restless and asking what was going on. Some came running over to the place where the eight foreigners were cowering. The Afghans who had accompanied them tried to calm the curious and send them away.

The helicopter flew repeatedly over the eight aid workers, but they were not detected. The situation was becoming more and more dangerous. There was, after all, a strict curfew, and the eight of them were just crouching down at the edge of a small free space which bordered the ruins of several houses. No wonder that it was becoming more restless in the city. Everyone could hear the ear-splitting sound of the helicopter. The helicopters could have been shot at. Afghans could have taken hold of the Shelter Now colleagues and handed them over to the Taliban.

"There's no point. The helicopters won't find you. Give in and come with me. People are beginning to notice you." The commander had suddenly turned up and was again pressuring Georg to give in. Each time the helicopter rumbled overhead, he would disappear quickly into the darkness and afterwards he would sit like a dragon behind them and try to persuade them.

"Georg, please don't give up. Give the Americans one more chance," pleaded Margrit and Dayna, who were sitting right beside him.

Georg Taubmann: The tension was becoming almost unbearable for me. Several times I was at the point of giving in to the commandant's pressure and going back to the house. But what then? What could we then have done? The whole city would have known that helicopters were there and that the foreigners were still in the city. The road route to Kabul was blocked, and it was only a matter of time till our captors were in the city again. Then we would have landed in Kandahar! And that would have been the end of us. We had to get into the helicopter, come what may. It was our only chance of survival!

I was on the verge of desperation and I cried, "God, please help us, please help us! Why are you allowing this?"

The rescue was so agonizingly close. We saw it and yet we couldn't reach it. The feelings which welled up in us cannot be described. I felt like a drowning man in the sea when a ship sails past. He shouts and waves, but the people don't see him and they sail right on by. His strength leaves him and he sinks into the abyss.

Silke Dürrkopf: It was bitterly cold and it seemed to me as if we would crouch there for an eternity. In my thoughts I had a discussion with God: *God, it's now gone far enough. Now do something! We need a miracle, get us out of here!*

I noticed that Georg was close to having a breakdown after all he'd been through that day, so I prayed constantly for him. He needed our support. The Afghans went on and on arguing with him, trying to persuade him that he should give in and come back to the house. But under no circumstances was I prepared to turn back. What could we have done then? I just wanted to stay sitting here and finally be rescued. "Georg, don't give up! Let's stay sitting and wait for another round!" I requested of him.

Margrit Stebner: I had looked at my watch; when we arrived at the place it was 11:30 pm. When we eventually got into the helicopter it was 2 o'clock in the morning. That was an interminably long time. And it was the toughest thing I experienced in the three and a half months! We were sitting almost an hour in the cold before the helicopters even turned up.

And then they flew away over us and simply didn't see us. We were really desperate and were terribly afraid. It seemed to me that the whole city would be awakened by the racket. All the dogs in Ghazni were barking like mad.

At some point a helicopter came rumbling by and flew past very close above us, causing a great swirl of dust. I've never experienced anything like it—the volume of noise, the dirt in our faces—we were almost blown over. The helicopter flew over us at least five times. And we couldn't do anything—just pray. "God, let them come back again! Let them finally see us!" It was enough to drive you crazy!

"We must light a fire so that they can recognize us," Heather cried, and undid her chador. We soaked the cloth in some kerosene from the lamp, lit it and waved it wildly to and fro. The others followed her lead and lit more items of clothing. The Afghans that had come with us recognized what she was trying to do and brought pieces of wood from the surrounding rubble which provided kindling for a large fire.

Again a helicopter rumbled so frighteningly close to them that sparks from the fire flew into their faces. Heather's clothing caught fire. They yelled and waved. It flew away. The aid workers were almost paralyzed and at this moment most of them gave up hope of ever being rescued. How could it be that they flew past us, didn't see us and flew away again? It was unbelievable!

But this time the pilot had seen the large fire and recognized the people. For the eight of them it had seemed like an eternity. Then, at last, suddenly and totally unexpectedly, out of the darkness, black figures which looked like beings from another planet appeared.

"Do you speak English?" one of them asked, … and quickly counted them off.

"One, two, three…" He reached only seven. He didn't recognize Georg, who in the darkness looked like an Afghan with his kameez and his beard. After the misunderstanding was cleared up, the soldiers gave their instructions. The eight followed them as quickly as they could, running along beside the houses, then around the corner—and before they knew it, they were crouching in the interior of this huge Chinook helicopter. Everything around them was pitch black and ear-shattering. The monster took off. At last on the way to freedom!

Georg Taubmann: For me everything was going too slowly. I ran directly up to the helicopter, ahead of our rescuers. While doing so, I fell into a pothole, ran on and quickly jumped into the black monster. Then I banged into a metal wall and fell to the floor. Heather, who was running behind me, tumbled over the top of me. Dazed, I crawled further on all fours, but we had at last reached our goal.

When the helicopter rose into the air, it was like a dream for me. I had no longer believed that they would manage to get us out.

The feeling was indescribable. "I can't believe it! I can't believe it!" I kept celebrating over and over. The rotary blades were so loud that we couldn't talk to each other, so we just squatted dumbly on the floor. Exuberantly happy, Heather crawled over to me and shouted in my ear, "We're free! We've done it! We're flying!"

At 5 o'clock in the morning the helicopters safely reached an airfield in Pakistan, directly over the border with Afghanistan. The Shelter Now aid workers transferred into a waiting cargo plane and landed about 8 o'clock in Islamabad.

There they were joyfully welcomed by the parents of the American women and by the representatives of the individual embassies. And then the first press conferences began. The whole world was eager to hear about their experiences of the previous 105 days.

Afghanistan—Focus of International Interest

THE FIRST INTERNATIONAL CONFERENCE ON AFGHANISTAN

In 2001 the first Afghanistan Conference took place from November 27 to December 5 on the Petersberg in Königswinter near Bonn. This would be followed by many more in the succeeding years. This showed that many states were prepared to help Afghanistan to rebuild after the Taliban had been removed from power. At the first conference, four delegations of different Afghan factions and tribal leaders took part, with a total of 28 delegates.

The aim was to discuss the direction of travel for the reconstruction of Afghanistan. How would the transition government look and who would be President? Which governmental system should be introduced? How long should the transition government last? When would the first elections be held? On the basis of these resolutions a lot was set in motion and built up in the following years.

From the beginning of 2002, because of the collapse of Taliban rule and the new stability, hundreds of aid organizations came into the country. Suddenly Afghanistan was the subject of interest throughout the whole world and received much recognition and support. That lasted, however, only a few years.

Subsequently other countries—like Iraq aroused international interest (the Gulf war), and interest in Afghanistan waned. Added to that was the rising strength of the Taliban which from 2003 began to launch attacks from Pakistan on the government, the army and the police, and to undertake attacks on the civil population and aid organizations. Gradually many aid organizations ceased their activities.

Georg Taubmann: I followed the first Afghanistan conference near Bonn with great excitement. It began a few days after our release. I knew their decisions would affect our return to Afghanistan. The sudden interest and involvement of the world made me very happy. Back in Kabul I was able to observe the progress with my own eyes. Of course lots of money flowed in. So prices rose dramatically. For example, in the Taliban period our house cost 200 dollars a month. After that the rents in this sector of the city suddenly rose to 4,000 and later 6,000 dollars per month.

In the press one would read again and again that monies were being wasted or disappearing down dark holes. But less recognized were the facts that thousands of schools were built, that the universities were functioning again, and that worldwide partnerships with universities in western countries were set up. Various main highways from Kabul to Pakistan, Iran, and Uzbekistan were fully restored—later also the airport and countless houses.

During Taliban rule there were no TV programs, whereas in 2016 there were 150 radio broadcasters and over 50 TV stations. New currency was also introduced to replace the old inflationary Afghani. Previously a flat bread cost 10,000 afghanis and in the new currency only 10 afghanis.

I like to compare Afghanistan with the reconstruction of Germany after the Second World War. Germany was similarly destroyed, but we had experienced and clever people in government ministries, in the administration, among the judges and police (even though the Nazi past of many had to be dealt with). However, during the Taliban regime when we went to the Planning Ministry, we would ascertain that the minister responsible for all the aid organizations had no clue about planning. When we needed a signature from the Health Minister—for equipping a clinic for example—then that was usually done with a thumbprint as the Minister couldn't write. All the ministries, like the Health Ministry, the Ministry of Education, the Courts, etc., had been occupied by uneducated and incompetent Taliban functionaries. With the setting up of the transitional government, these had to be newly established and occupied. How could that happen when the majority of educated Afghans had fled abroad under Taliban terror? That demanded a large amount of patient rebuilding work. The Germans appointed the police force and educated the Afghan policemen. Whenever we arrived at the airport, a German policeman would usually be standing there with an Afghan policeman. That's how they were trained. Only when one considers all this can one appreciate all that has been achieved in Afghanistan.

I was busy working on corrections to the manuscript *Escape from Kabul* with Georg Taubmann, when a telephone call interrupted us. A friend from Afghanistan was calling him.

"Mr. George, yesterday I slaughtered a cow and three sheep and have invited all the local tribal leaders from the region of Khost to a great celebration," the voice said in broken English. "All of them have spoken highly about Shelter Now and would like you and your people to come back soon to Afghanistan to our province.

At the end of the celebration we drafted a letter. Twelve tribal princes have signed it. They invite you to start up your aid projects in our province. I am sending you the invitation very soon."

A few days later we held the letter in our hands. Georg personally knew most of the tribal leaders who had signed. Shelter Now had produced more than 100,000 concrete roof girders in this province and passed them on to the population at a greatly subsidized price. One of the signatories had indeed been at the Afghanistan Conference at Petersberg in Bonn.

An Excerpt from the Letter Wednesday, 9-1-2002
(see photograph of the letter on next page)

To Shelter Now, Germany

Many, many greetings from the tribal leaders in the Province of Khost to the Director of Shelter Now, Mr George.

For a long time in our province we have had your project (a factory for concrete roof girders) which was very helpful for our people. Unfortunately this project was demolished by the Taliban and closed down, which is very sad for us.

We tribal leaders have decided to issue a formal invitation to Shelter Now. Please help us to rebuild our province as soon as possible.

We esteem the German people highly for all the help in the past and we know Mr. George to be a noble and helpful person. He can help us more than anyone else because he knows our culture and our problems very well. It pains us that Mr.

George had so many difficulties and was imprisoned. We were very unhappy that we were unable to assist him.

We now sign this letter with the highest respect for Mr. George and Shelter Now.

RISE AND FALL OF THE TALIBAN

December 6, 2001, is regarded as the day on which the Taliban were finally defeated and driven out of Afghanistan. Their Supreme Leader Mullah Omar with his trusty followers withdrew to Pakistan from their bastion in Kandahar in the south, the place where they had first come on the scene in 1994. There they licked their wounds and regrouped.

In 2003 they reappeared for the first time. From the beginning of 2006, they carried out increased attacks against Afghan civilians or soldiers of the ISAF[4]. The Taliban directed their attacks specifically at the Afghan civilian population and at foreigners. According to United Nations statements, in the year 2009 they were responsible for over 76% of victims among Afghan civilians.

Wednesday January 9, 2002

To Shelter ~~Know~~ International

Germany

Many many greetings from Khost tribal leaders to head of Shelter now international (Mr. George) From along ago there was your project of Guarders, which was lead by shelter now International And these project was very Helpful to Khost people, As you have information that Afghans people Have seen many problems and suffered in many fighting, but It was very helpful Project for Khost Tribal people. But we re get to say that this project was looted and was closed by Taliban and It was dark age . but nowadays situation is very excellent than anyother time and today we have a big Meeting in Khost about your project. And we have decided today to Invite formally shelter now International to take part in the rehabilitation of Khost province, we suggest for you to open a project in Khost as soon as possible and also we love germen people very much. Because they have Served to khost people very well, before also there were a lot of projects and now also, but we know Mr. George Head of shelter now and he is a kind, noble and helpful person and we know him very well and he can work better than anyother person and project, because he is familiar with our culture we would like German people very much and they know our problems very well and they can work better that anyother people. And we hope that you will never forget Afghans people . Especially Khost people.

It is true that you have seen many difficulties and you were in Jail. And we were very very unhappy , but we couldn't help you on that time. Because the first people were khost people. Against of Taliban and now we will sign these letters. We love Mr.Goerge very much .

Love to Mr.Goerge a head of shelter now International and German People.

1. Sayder Jan
2. Haji Shaswer Khan (Tanai)
3. Naeem (Kochai)
4. Haji Wazir (Mangal)
5. Abdul Qayoom Khan
6. Mirbadod (Tanai)
7. Shah Khan (GurBuz)
8. Dr.Mohammad Din Gul
9. Haji Sher Gul (GurBuz)
10. Deputy Governor of Khost Province Mustafa (Khostwal).
11. Governor of Khost Badshah -Khan (Jadran)
12. Speaker of khost showra and province (Khostwall)

Invitation from the twelve tribal princes to start up aid projects in their province

The withdrawal of the ISAF at the end of 2014 and the increase in attacks by the Taliban led to great insecurity among the foreign aid organisations. Also attacks on foreigners increased. For security reasons more and more aid organisations pulled out of Afghanistan.

The Afghan Taliban movement had its origins in Pakistan. Everyone who has been instructed in the so-called madrassas (conservative Koran schools) in the radical Sunni tradition is addressed in Arabic as *Talib* (student of religion) or plural *Taliban*. [p71]

During an eight-year basic education, one learns in a madrassa everything about becoming a mullah (title given to an Islamic priest and scholar). Many Pashtun refugee families from Afghanistan sent their sons to these schools, as they were provided with clothing and food. Besides religious instruction—in which less of the Koran and more of sharia is emphasized—the boys were also given a military education. Reading and writing seemed not so important, hence the high number of Illiterates among the Taliban.

Mullah Omar got involved in the power struggles of the various groups of the mujahideen (God's warriors) in Afghanistan. In 1994 they appeared for the first time in the southern city of Kandahar. They spread out quickly and in September 1996 captured the capital, Kabul, proclaiming the Islamic Emirate of Afghanistan. The Taliban extended their influence until around 90% of Afghanistan was under their control. Mullah Mohammed Omar set up a thinly veiled religious dictatorship on the basis of sharia, the Islamic Divine Law from the early Middle Ages. He declared that he had created the purest Islamic State in the world.

The henchmen of the religious and cultural police patrolled the streets of Kabul daily. Women who were not sufficiently veiled were struck with leather whips. They controlled men's haircuts and the length of their beards. They closed shops whose owners did not attend the mosque regularly. They beat the men to go to prayer. They whipped women as well as men for minor misdemeanors. Hands and feet were amputated for theft.

September 11 will go down in the history of the USA as an unforgettably tragic day. Early in the morning four commercial aircraft were hijacked. Two were diverted into the towers of the World Trade Center (WTC) in New York City and one into the Pentagon in Arlington (Virginia). The fourth aircraft, probably with the further goal of attacking Washington, D.C., was brought down over Shanksville in Pennsylvania by the hijackers during struggles with passengers. At least 2,993 people met their death in the WTC. Approximately 15,100 persons were able to flee the WTC towers before it collapsed.

US citizens were in a state of shock. The perpetrators were sought urgently. Soon members of Al Qaeda were identified as the main culprits, who had their base in the Taliban Emirate and were linked to the Taliban. The leader was Osama bin Laden who was henceforth the most hunted man in the world. On September 19, US President George W. Bush demanded of the Taliban regime that they hand over Osama bin Laden "immediately and without conditions," as well as the eight hostages, among whom were two US citizens. Otherwise they would have to reckon on military consequences. The Taliban refused and prepared for a military offensive.

The US forces prepared their military operation, set up support bases in Pakistan and made their aircraft carriers ready. Beginning October 7, 2001, they intervened militarily in Afghanistan under the name Operation Enduring Freedom. They

> Concerning the eight development workers, from now on they were officially known only as hostages. The US Government had clearly come to the conclusion that their capture on the pretext of supposed proselytizing had been long planned in order to use them as hostages in any negotiations.

supported ground troops of the Northern Alliance with massive air attacks in a major offensive against the Taliban and bombed strategic targets in Kabul: military installations, public buildings and the houses of Taliban leaders. The collapse of the Taliban forces, which had 90% of the country under their control, progressed quickly. In the north and the northeast a new city was taken almost every day. Then came Herat, and on November 14, the Northern Alliance, supported by US military forces, reached the outskirts of Kabul. The city was taken without a struggle on the day that the aid workers were captured from the prison. The eventual victory over the Taliban regime was the collapse of the city of Kandahar.

International Security Assistance Force (ISAF)

The United Nations assured the Afghan transitional government in Kabul of support in rebuilding and on December 20, 2001, decided on the dispatch of the military mission ISAF to Afghanistan. It was ISAF's brief to secure a safe environment in the country for the work of Afghan institutions and international organizations. The ISAF cooperated militarily with the Afghan security forces against Taliban fighters and other insurgents. Another of their tasks was to train the Afghan security forces.

The first ISAF soldiers arrived in Afghanistan in January 2002. Initially their sphere of operations was confined to Kabul and the surrounding area, but from 2003 this was expanded to cover the whole country. Since August 2003, the ISAF was under the command of NATO. In 2009 the NATO states decided on a massive build-up of ISAF troops due to the worsening security situation. By the end of 2010, around 130,000 ISAF soldiers from 48 countries were stationed in Afghanistan. From the beginning, Germany was one of the highest contributors to the ISAF troops.

In spite of continuing violence, the NATO countries decided at their summit in Lisbon in November 2010 that responsibility for security in Afghanistan up to the end of 2014 should be handed over to the local security forces. From July 2011, the NATO countries gradually withdrew their soldiers and material assistance from Afghanistan. From January 1, 2015 around 12,000 NATO soldiers were to train, advise and support the Afghan security forces, but no longer be involved militarily.

This number was increased little by little in 2017/2018 as the Afghan security forces were seen to be over-stretched and the NATO training mission too small. Reasons given were the increasing strength of radical Islamic Taliban and the spread of the terrorist militia Islamic State (IS).

LOOKING BACK: BOMBS AND PRAYERS

On that tragic September 11, 2001 the Shelter Now aid workers had already been imprisoned for 40 days. While the US forces were preparing militarily for an act of reprisal, the nervousness of the Taliban increased day by day and the tension between the eight foreigners and the Taliban guards grew, especially towards the two men. This intensified when the US military forces finally began their attacks on October 7. One of the guards remarked aggressively, "If we have to flee from here, then we'll kill the foreigners first."

Some nights, Georg Taubmann and Peter Bunch could scarcely sleep, as they knew that the harder the Taliban were hit, the more dangerous they became.

Georg compared some to wild animals which, when wounded, react all the more unpredictably. For this reason the two men didn't go out into the prison yard on days with especially skilled shooters around, just in case.... The aggressive mood could have been discharged on them.

The prison supervisor, Mullah Hamid, who had sympathy for the foreigners, was very concerned for their safety. More than once he said to Georg, "Mr. George, I am afraid that the dreaded Taliban from Kandahar, the Al Qaeda fighters, will find out that you are here and will take you captive or take revenge on you. And then I don't know how I can protect you."

Day 66: October 7, 2001
Excerpt from the book Escape from Kabul

It all started on a Sunday afternoon. Georg Taubmann and Peter Bunch were doing their rounds of the prison yard, when suddenly in Kabul many guns were firing. It was mainly anti-aircraft fire but there were also individual Kalashnikovs shooting into the air, because a single small aircraft was circling overhead—obviously a reconnaissance plane.

The senseless detonation of munitions was surely the release of the enormous tension that had increasingly built up in the Taliban over the previous weeks.

Every day they were expecting the promised reprisal by the US forces, as day by day the encirclement of Afghanistan grew tighter and tighter. In Pakistan and Uzbekistan, troops were at the ready, aircraft carriers were anchored in the Indian Ocean, prepared for action. And no one knew where, when and how hard the troops would strike. All waited in suspense and dread.

For a whole four and a half weeks the "Alliance against Terror" took time to prepare for the counter attack, which left the nerves of the Taliban in shreds.

Georg Taubmann: As soon as the shooting started, I asked if I could be allowed to go across to the women. Fortunately I was given permission. "The bombing on the part of the US Alliance hasn't begun yet," I reassured them. It's only a reconnaissance plane flying over Kabul and the Taliban are acting crazy. But tonight it could take off. Let's pray that God protects us and that the Americans know where we are." We had received tips that were to be taken seriously that the American forces knew where we were and would really try to spare us during their attacks.

As I had suspected, the bombing of specific targets in Kabul did indeed begin that same night. During this time we men were incarcerated up on the first floor. If the prison had been hit, not one of us would have escaped. We would all have been killed. Nevertheless, among the prisoners there was more joy than fear, as for many the beginning of the war meant the justified hope of release.

"We're praying five times a day to Allah, that this regime will be destroyed," declared some of my fellow prisoners over and over again.

The crashing of the bombs and the ensuing explosions broke over Kabul in waves. Many areas in the city were illuminated and the hits were so powerful that sometimes the whole building shook. We ran from one side of the windows to the other and watched what was happening all around us.

The second night was even more fierce, as the planes struck at targets quite close to us. The noise was powerful, the walls shook so much that at times it took my breath away. Especially when I looked at the barricaded steel door and was aware that there was no escape. It was like being in a highly explosive cage.

Quite close to us there must have been a very powerful hit, for the building shook as in an earthquake and through the windows the explosion made it as bright as day. The next morning we learned that the tower of Radio Sharia right beside us had taken a single precise hit.

Another night the radar installation and the TV tower were demolished. The tower had stood like a symbol on a hill in the center of Kabul. When we looked out the window the following morning, we saw how the whole top of the hill had been sliced off as if with a knife. No tower, no radar installation were to be seen.

Through a foreign broadcaster we later discovered that the woman pilot who had carried out this brilliant achievement was honoured personally by President Bush. For the Taliban it was particularly annoying that a woman had destroyed their symbol. In Kabul a woman was not even allowed to drive a car and now a woman pilot, of all people, had blown away a tower which was so significant for them.

Katrin Jelinek: I didn't find the first night of bombing so bad, as the sound of war had begun in the afternoon with the din of the defense artillery. As well, Georg and Peter had fortunately been able to come across to us to explain the situation. In the evening the signal rockets went off, which reminded me very much of New Year's Eve. We stood outside and watched the spectacle. The real bombardment didn't go off till late in the night when we were already asleep.

The second night however was really fierce, as the bombs fell very close to us. That's why we all—except Silke—moved into the corridor, where there were no windows. During these hours I was really afraid. With the many swishing sounds, the loud explosions and the floor shaking, I got awful cramps in my stomach. At night it's much worse than by day for then you can at least see what's going on around you. I kept praying, "Oh Lord, spare us! Please bring us out of here unharmed!"

Margrit Stebner: I lay with the others in the corridor and looked at the walls, where there were already lots of cracks. Basically it wouldn't take another bomb to fall on our prison, it only needed to have a good shake and everything would collapse.

When more and more bombs then fell and landed near us, I was seized with panic. "Oh, God, what shall I do?" went through my mind. "I can't run away. I cannot get out of here!"

At that moment, it seemed as if someone nudged me and said, "Stay calm. Just turn over and go to sleep. It'll all be okay!"

God was there the whole night! That brought me great relief. I am firmly convinced that you can't imagine something like that. Either you experience it and can stay calm or you crack up.

After the American Air Force had specifically attacked and destroyed the most important military targets, they concentrated on the Taliban's line of defense against the Northern Alliance, which at this point lay about 30 kilometers north of Kabul near Shamalie. The prisoners heard the airplanes roaring over their prison and the dull rumble of the impact of the bombs.

What especially appalled the Taliban was the appearance of an airplane out of a clear blue sky targeting a specific building, shooting it to pieces, and then disappearing again. The precision with which groups of Taliban leaders were eliminated baffled them and created fear and horror.

In the coming weeks up to their abduction to Kandahar, the eight hostages were often taken during the night to another high security prison, the dreaded Riasat 3. For a period this occurred every night, but sometimes only every second or third night. At about 6 o'clock in the evening they were taken there and brought back again at about 7 o'clock the next morning. Why that happened, the eight could only guess. One reason could be that in the high security prison they were safer from the nightly bombing. It was however highly possible that the Taliban feared that a special commando of the US forces could try to free them by force.

Day 81: October 21, 2001

In their cell Georg Taubmann and Peter Bunch were getting ready for the evening when Georg was suddenly called down to the office. Rather surprised by what this call at this time of day might mean, he went down the dark corridor. In the office, Mullah Hamid, the head of the prison, and his boss, Mullah Yussuf, the most hated man in the prison, awaited him. The latter began to speak: "Pack your things! You're being taken to another prison tonight."

Again he was applying these inconsiderate tactics and Georg had to try hard not to let his fear show. "How come that we have to leave here? What's all this?" he protested.

"We're taking you to a better place. As well, it's safer, especially because of the bombs at night."

Georg didn't believe this pack of lies and replied, "We don't need a better place. It's fine here. We want to stay here."

At this, Mullah Yussuf became aggressive and answered sharply, "Who is it makes the decisions here? Who gives the orders? You or me?"

"You, of course!"

"Then fetch your things and see to it that you get down here!"

After this interchange, Georg thought it wiser to give in and told Peter. They quickly packed a few of their things together and then locked the cell door from outside with a padlock. When they left their prison wing they felt very uneasy. They worried, *What are they doing with us now? Where are they taking us to?*

As strange as it may seem, this prison had become something of a "home" for them in the past five weeks. They had built up relationships, knew the guards, knew how the system functioned and felt to a certain extent safe. Also the Afghan prisoners had assured them repeatedly that they would protect them should it come to attacks by radical Taliban. Some had even said, "If the Northern Alliance fighters free us, you can sneak through along with us. Our homes are nearby."

Now they were horrified and wondered, "What are they going to do with the foreigners?" Their friend Mohammed Sharif walked part way along the corridor with them, distraught, and then stopped, his shoulders drooping. He could not support them. Again everything was uncertain and dangerous. They were hostages without rights, without support.

When the two men got into the minibus together with the women, terror was written across their faces too. They likewise did not believe the assurances of the guards that they were being taken away for only one night and had packed all their sparse belongings.

As the one with the best local knowledge Georg paid special attention to the way the convoy went. The route went through the city center; first past the Turkish Embassy, then the Chinese Embassy. After that they drove around a bend and stopped beside the former GDR Embassy, in front of the infamous Riasat-3 prison of the secret service. There they had to get out and were again separated from each other. The women were taken to the first floor of the building and the men were led into the basement.

Georg Taubmann: Peter and I were led along a dark corridor that ended at a large steel door. Behind it steps led down into the basement. What awaited us there was the worst that I have ever experienced. The first prisoners that we saw had completely expressionless, sad faces. Clearly, many of them were severely traumatized or mentally disturbed. The twitches in their faces, the emptiness in their eyes—we were confronted with unadulterated hopelessness. It took my breath away. The atmosphere was indescribable. The air was damp and cold, many of the men sick and suffering from shock. The fact that we were stuck in a cell under the ground even caused me—I who could cope with a lot—claustrophobia for the very first time. Above us near the ceiling, there was a small shaft, which let in light from outside one meter under ground level.

Bewildered, we squatted down on our mattresses. We probably looked just like the prisoners who were staring at us. Two of the inmates, who had not been quite so affected as the others, saw that we were in a state of shock. They were concerned for us. One of them introduced himself as Mustafa, a clever man I would soon find out, with whom I quickly became friends. He made some tea and described the prison to us. It was one of the many high security prisons of the secret service.

"In Kabul there is Riasat 1 right up to Riasat 12," he explained to us. "There are many here who are condemned to death; others are awaiting the punishment of amputation. Most of them are innocent prisoners—only a few have committed a crime. And in this prison there is a wing which is considerably worse than this one here."

Peter and I were in despair. We squatted in the cell not knowing what to say. Fortunately, earlier that day, before being driven here, we had received mail. "I'll read my letters," I said to myself, "to distract my thoughts."

There were some letters from Marianne, who was now so far away from me. Until recently I had thought she was in Pakistan with the children, but they had had to flee to Germany due to the great danger. At that moment, as I thought it all over, the total wretchedness of our situation overwhelmed me. It was dreadful to know that she was so far away across the globe. In the first letter she told me that her stepfather had had an accident, in the second that he was lying in a coma, and in the third I learned that he was dead and buried. How had Marianne survived that? How would she be able to comfort her mother? And my boys? For them it was the first time that any of our relatives had died. What would have gone through their heads at the funeral when they thought of their own father?

This thought troubled me. I no longer knew what I should do. I opened my Bible and began to read. My eyes landed on Psalm 91: "You will not fear the terror by night… For you have said, the Lord is my refuge! He commands his angels to guard you in all your ways." These words comforted me enormously. After I had read them several times, Peter and I prayed together for our families and poured out our hearts to God. In the night I could not sleep despite two sleeping tablets, as the smells and the sounds around me were too strange and too sinister. On my arrival I had seen to my horror that among the prisoners there were men bound with chains. While I was dozing, the rattling, scratching sounds of their tiny steps in the corridor pursued me.

The morning came and time dragged on without our being picked up. "Did the Taliban actually deceive us? Must we really stay in this dreadful prison?"

Georg Taubmann and Peter Bunch paced the corridor restlessly. "Oh God, get us out of here!" they both prayed in despair. "We can't bear it. We'll become as crazy as the other prisoners if we have to stay here! Please change the hearts of the Taliban so that they come and get us!"

At last, toward 11 o'clock the guards came and ordered them abruptly, "Get your things and come with us!"

For Georg and Peter it was almost as if they'd been set free. Back in the old prison they were surrounded at once by the other prisoners, who were delighted to have them back again. It was like a homecoming!

Margrit Stebner: Riasat 3 was a men's prison. At night we were the only women there, accommodated on the first floor. Actually, it was an office wing, sealed off at the entrance by a large door with a grille. We had two rooms—a small one for Silke and Katrin and a larger one for the rest of us four women. As it was already the end of October, it was bitterly cold at night, because the window panes were broken and only a sheet of plastic provided any protection.

In the hallway there was always a male guard sitting, which we found disgraceful. So we protested so long till we got a padlock, with which we locked the door from inside.

The atmosphere in this building was creepy, which left me unable to sleep at night.

Added to that was the host of bats that flew around screeching in front of our window. You can't properly describe the sound: sometimes it sounded like a baby's cry, sometimes like a high, ugly screech.

There on the first floor the nightly bombing was quite threatening, as there would have been no escape for us if a bomb had hit. But I wouldn't have wanted to sleep in the basement either, like Georg and Peter.

When I think back on it, this gloomy atmosphere and the bats were really awful.

Georg Taubmann: Whenever Peter and I were brought back to the high security prison in the evening, our two prison friends were waiting for us. As soon as they heard our vehicle, Mustafa put on the kettle and we would squat down beside each other till late into the night and chat.

Only after two weeks did I trust myself to explore this sinister wing of the prison further. Immediately on the left when one came down the stairs, a dark corridor went even deeper underground. Once I dared to go in there and discovered that the prisoners were housed in small cells for six. On each side of these rooms were three self-made bedsteads of wooden planks, built on top of each other. Above them was a small skylight through which a little light filtered. But mostly it was dark—the electricity often failed. How did people endure it in these dungeons for months on end? Many of them coughed constantly in the clammy air; some had tuberculosis.

And there were still other cells in which men were cooped up in threes and were only permitted out morning and evening for a short trip to the toilet. Many of them wore foot-chains, which meant they could only take very short steps. A further piece of chain had been attached to the middle of the foot-chain, the end of which was held by the prisoner. He pulled this end piece up with his hands, so that he could more easily place one foot in front of the other when walking, and the foot-chain didn't drag so loudly along the ground. The whole gloomy scene reminded me of the dungeons in the Middle Ages.

Sometime earlier, my young friend Mohammed Sharif had got me a small radio with earphones from the bazaar. I always carried it around carefully concealed on my person. Whenever we arrived in our night prison, we shut ourselves in our cell with Mustafa and secretly listened to the news from foreign broadcasters. We had to be very careful when doing this, so as not to be discovered, as there were Taliban informers among the prisoners. Mustafa had previously served in the army and was well informed on the whole geography of Afghanistan. He explained to us where fighting was going on and which cities had been taken by the Northern Alliance supported by US forces. Cleverly he drew a map of Afghanistan, put in the different cities and explained the battlegrounds to us. A very decisive event was the conquest of the strongly disputed city of Mazar-i-Sharif in the North of the country. From this point on the troop movements of the Northern Alliance proceeded apace.

The following night we found out that the next city had been captured and then the next and the next. Within a few days practically the whole of the north had been taken, right down to Herat. We sat mesmerized in front of the little radio and listened to the news of victory. Then when the Taliban lines in the north of Kabul in Shamalie district were attacked, we were sure that it would only take a few days for the Northern Alliance to march into Kabul.

I took notes every night and whenever we were driven back to our day prison in the morning, I secretly slipped the others these notes. After breakfast they could then read their "newspaper."

On one of the following days in late afternoon there was suddenly unrest in the day prison. The guards were running up and down nervously, they were irritated, and there was aggressive tension in the air.

Just as some soup was about to be brought across from the women's prison to Georg Taubmann and Peter Bunch, Mullah Hamid and his boss, Mullah Yussuf, suddenly stormed into the cell and ordered: "Let's go, get up! We must take you immediately to the night prison."

"What's the big hurry? We haven't eaten yet."

"Then take your soup with you! We've got to leave immediately!"

The two men had no other choice than to obey and in great haste they were packed into the minibus with the women and taken to the night-time prison earlier than usual. On arriving there Georg and Peter stumbled down the dark stairs to their basement dungeon where an excited Mustafa awaited them.

"Nearly there," he informed them. "This afternoon I heard in the news that the troops of the Northern Alliance have begun their attack on the Shamalie front lines and are now advancing on Kabul. They're only 10 kilometers away. It can't be long before they're in the city."

The excitement among the prisoners was enormous; they ran restlessly to and fro in the corridors. How would the conquest of Kabul turn out? Would they be rescued by the Northern Alliance troops or would the guards kill some of them first? Those who had been condemned to death especially dreaded this fate. And what would happen to the captured aid workers?

Then heavily armed Taliban stormed the prison intending to drag them off to Kandahar, to the stronghold of the Al Qaeda militia and the residence of Mullah Mohammed Omar—obviously in order to extort concessions from the American Forces.

Return—Obstacles in the Way

Georg's thoughts were often with the suffering people of Afghanistan—too often to allow him to relax there in Germany. He felt the urge to return, now that the immediate threat had lessened due to the collapse of the Taliban regime. He was happy about the written invitation from the tribal leader of Khost province. It had reached him at the beginning of January 2002 and showed how necessary their assistance in rebuilding was. He drew up plans as to how reconstruction could succeed, and prayed a lot.

First of all Georg wanted to know who of the colleagues were prepared to continue leading the work in Pakistan or to rebuild in Afghanistan with him. All the western Shelter Now workers had left Afghanistan and Pakistan and were scattered all over the world. The work in Pakistan, especially in the large refugee camps, had continued to be led in their absence by reliable local colleagues. But even they could do with encouragement and support. So Georg sent out a circular letter with the invitation to come to a discussion about the situation in Swat, North Pakistan. They would talk about the essentials. He set the date for April 2002. He was interested to see who would come.

TO PAKISTAN–DESPITE ENTRY BAN

At this time there were still no direct flights to Afghanistan. One had to fly via Pakistan. So Georg applied for a visa for himself and his family at the Pakistani Embassy in Berlin. There was of course an old story concerning the refusal of an entry visa for Georg but he thought that would have expired long ago. The tickets were booked for a Monday. On Saturday morning the passports came back— without any visa stamp. Visas were not granted. Over the weekend nothing could be done, but early Monday morning Marianne rushed to the residents' registration office and applied for three temporary passes for herself and the two boys. Georg had a second passport.

Georg Taubmann: I hadn't reckoned at all on my visa being refused. I thought the affair was water under the bridge.

> During his time as leader of Shelter Now in Pakistan, Georg Taubmann appointed an Afghan who was living in the refugee camp to undertake increasingly responsible tasks. Among these was the responsibility for distributing foodstuffs to refugees. After some time Georg found out that he was misappropriating large quantities of foodstuff. He was caught in the act and called to account. Things went back and forth, but eventually it was no longer feasible to keep this colleague and he had to be dismissed. The man came from one of the most dangerous Afghan tribes who were well known for their criminal activities. His honor was severely wounded by this dismissal. He went back to his tribe and a short time later declared his animosity and revenge towards Georg.
>
> He had also threatened Georg physically. He sought out different embassies. He went to the UN as well and to the Pakistani secret police and spread the most evil stories about Georg. Such as, Georg had offered him money to convert to Christianity. That was of course one of the most slanderous accusations, whereupon the Pakistani Government did not extend Georg's visa and he had to leave the country on its expiry. Thereafter he was on the blacklist.

But how could I get back to Kabul if not via Pakistan? I refused to be deterred and doggedly followed my plans. We just made it in time in our car to Munich airport. Silke was travelling with us; she wanted to go back to Kabul to teach our boys. I negotiated with the airline—but without a visa there was no permission to fly to Pakistan. They allowed us to fly only as far as Dubai and we postponed our onward flight to Pakistan by three days. I then intended to apply for the visa in Dubai.

The next morning I rush to the Pakistani embassy. The embassy official looks at our papers. "I cannot give you a visa, as you have no residence permit for Dubai. Sorry. You should have seen to this in Berlin." He pushes the papers back to me.

"But listen," I begin with oriental politeness, "I have worked for 16 years in Pakistan. Both of my splendid sons were born in your country in Peshawar and feel at home there. They are practically Pakistanis. Really, they should have a Pakistani passport. May I ask, where is your home in Pakistan?"

"I come from Rawalpindi."

"What, from Rawalpindi! I know the city well. We have visited it many times. It would be such a shame if we couldn't return to that wonderful country. Can you not grant us a visa?"

The conversation must have impressed him so much that he began to work on our applications without even checking our data on the computer. "I'll see what I can do. Come back in three days. Then everything should be ready."

"Oh, can you not do it in two days? You know, we have already got our flight tickets and they'll become invalid."

"No, impossible. My colleagues require at least three days."

"But you are a man of authority and have such great influence here. " At that he felt so flattered that by the next morning I had all the visas in my hand and nothing more stood in the way of our flight to Islamabad.

But the tension wasn't over yet. *What will happen at Immigration when they look at the computer and see that I'm still on the blacklist?* I went quite slowly and stood quite far back in the queue, hoping that the border officials would become less diligent by the end. When I noticed that in front of me every single person was being photographed and all data meticulously typed into the computer, I felt queasy. *How am I to get through here trouble-free? And what if they send me back or even arrest me?* I groaned softly. Sweat broke out on my forehead. Marianne, the boys, Silke—all knew the situation was critical. Spellbound, we watched the approaching queue and prayed quietly.

Then a man in civilian clothing approaches from behind, addresses us and asks us to follow him. *Oh, now they've caught me. What'll they do with me?* My stomach turns somersaults but I follow him. What else can I do? He goes to one of the desks that isn't manned. "Please give me your passports." I give him the whole bundle, plus Silke's passport. He opens each one, searches for the page with the visa, stamps in the entry permission and his signature below it. He doesn't bother with the computer beside him. He kindly waves us through and tells us we may go straight to the baggage area. While waiting at the luggage X-ray machine we are again waved through. I can scarcely take it in and have to ensure that my mouth doesn't stay open!

Silke observes all this and remarks drily, "Tell me, I suppose you have your connections everywhere. Was that another of your friends?"

"I've never seen that man. I don't know him, have never met him," I reply, totally perplexed. And there we were, in Pakistan!

Marianne Taubmann: For Georg it was clear right from his time in prison that he would go back, if he got out alive. For the German women it was similar. For me too, it was the same. So we didn't need to have big discussions. And yet it wasn't so easy for me, as one simply doesn't know what's in store. For that reason it was good to go back initially to a familiar setting and to our friends in Pakistan. We wanted to meet with our colleagues there and consult each other as to how to proceed. From the start the boys looked forward to their friends and familiar surroundings. Naturally there were overtones of fear about going back, but somehow I knew in my heart that we were going. The fact that we were together again as a family and could talk about it and that others wanted to return brought a certain inner peace. As I said, it was enormously helpful to gather together again in Pakistan.

STAFF GET-TOGETHER IN SWAT

Approximately 15 people found their way to the meeting slightly north of Peshawar. Finally seeing each other again was a great joy. Greg Gilmore, who had previously led the work in Pakistan, had been with relatives in Europe in the meantime and came with his family. After the attack on the World Trade Center in New York on September 11, 2001, he and his family and all the other western colleagues had to leave Pakistan for security reasons. Life became extremely dangerous for them there. Len and Diane Stitt, who had earlier led the team in Afghanistan, also appeared. In a hazardous venture after the arrest of the eight Shelter Now aid workers, Len had led the rest of the team out by road and into Pakistan. For an American that was extremely risky, as the Taliban wanted to get their hands on as many US citizens as possible. Now both of them had returned and were prepared to continue the work in Afghanistan with Georg and his family. Likewise, Silke and another American woman. Also present were the founder of Shelter Now, Douglas Layton, who had begun the development work in 1983, and Udo Stolte, leader of Shelter Now Germany.

At this meeting it wasn't just about the resumption of the work in Afghanistan, but also about again supporting the projects in Pakistan which had been kept going by local staff and undertaking new projects. Over and above all this, it was important for everyone to find their bearings and to reorient themselves.

Everyone had been shaken by the past crisis and had to reorganize themselves again. The beautiful mountainous landscape in Swat valley was exactly the right setting.

Georg Hits Burnout

On the one hand, Georg was happy to see his colleagues not only doing well, but also still full of enthusiasm to continue working with him; on the other hand, he sensed a strong lack of motivation and a powerful need for rest and sleep. At night he was plagued with nightmares and during the day he sometimes didn't want to see anyone. Classic signs of burnout. For the outside observer, that was almost to be expected. Georg always lived on the edge. It was difficult to give him advice or to get him to slow down. The strains and trauma of imprisonment were only four months behind him.

Georg Taubmann: I have always really pushed myself, rushing from one engagement to the next. Yes, there was the joyous expectation of seeing my colleagues and the new beginning in Afghanistan; but then worry and anxiety would suddenly overwhelm me. How could all this be achieved? The stress of getting into Pakistan without an entry visa must also have gnawed away at me. The more concrete our plans, the more difficult I found it emotionally.

And then, at this get-together in Swat, it simply threw me for a loop. I had never before experienced anything to this degree. I remembered what the professionals in France had told us about the stages of burnout and its symptoms—and that these could show up much later. I recognized this now in myself. As a rule I didn't need very much sleep, but suddenly I was extremely tired and could sleep for hours. I had no energy, and I couldn't concentrate properly. I sat in the meetings but got very little out of them. Normally I work out exactly who I want to sit beside at mealtimes to have a discussion with or who I want to spend time with during the breaks. And what was I doing now? I slipped past the dining hall so as not to be recognized. In our room, I lay down on the bed right away to rest. Then I dragged myself into the next session and tried to participate as best I could.

After the get-together, we went back to Peshawar. Udo Stolte spent a few more days with us. He was full of enthusiasm about the outcome of the meeting and the continuation of the work in Afghanistan. He urged me to take a short trip to Kabul in order to see how the situation was there. Everything within me resisted. "I can't, Udo," I said. "I simply don't have the strength." I sensed only this great weariness.

This lasted for quite a while. Even after we were in Kabul, I was still suffering.

Marianne Taubmann: I did not know *this* Georg. In our 19 years of marriage, I had never experienced anything like it. I was concerned and shocked. Georg is otherwise a real extrovert who is always talking to someone or other, during breaks or at meals, is always making plans, meeting with colleagues... Now, suddenly, he was completely different. It was totally strange to me that suddenly he didn't want to see anyone and just slouched in our room. I had to entice him out of the room every mealtime. I felt helpless and insecure and didn't know how to deal with it. I simply knew that it must be burnout. I complied with his wishes and did what he said. I would fetch him this and that, but he didn't wish to see or speak to anyone. He just came to the meetings and then disappeared again. He just wanted to be on his own, to meditate and pray. "Simply get some peace"—those were his words. That was very, very disconcerting for me. It made me afraid.

Back in Peshawar we had something like a management meeting with Udo. Udo suggested enthusiastically: "Let's go across to Afghanistan again and see how it is there and meet up with Len…" Georg was completely against it and not in a state to start anything new and face the challenges. Then I knew we needed some time. We just need some leisure time, to find ourselves again and to get clarity. Just ordinary daily life. Gradually, Georg met up again with his colleagues and the Afghans in Peshawar. But that was with no time pressure and without having constantly to make important decisions. It was of course helpful that in the team we met every day for prayer. We were about two months in Pakistan and Georg suffered burnout for almost the whole period. Slowly he recovered and was able to dare to return to Kabul.

Udo Stolte: During the get-together in Swat, Georg was scarcely to be seen or to be spoken to. He came to the main functions, was there for meals and disappeared immediately afterwards. That's when I thought, *Man, he must be at the end of his tether.* After the get-together, I spent a few more days in Peshawar with him and Marianne. I was full of energy and would dearly have loved to take a quick trip to Kabul to sound out the situation there. Georg had a close Afghan friend who had links to Karsai, the transitional president. Deepening contact now and meeting the people could only be advantageous for Shelter Now. But no, Georg reacted negatively to the topic of Kabul and withdrew into his shell.

Friends in Peshawar

Georg Taubmann: In Peshawar I had a very, very encouraging experience. By this time we had lived and worked in Peshawar for 16 years and through the years very close friendships had been formed with Pakistani Christians and also Muslim families. It was a huge intercultural family. One of the Pakistani Christian Churches was especially very close to us. While we were in prison, they had prayed a lot for us, and now that we were again in Peshawar, they arranged a huge celebration for us in one of their church halls. It lasted the whole day. They continually wanted to hear the story about our capture, how we were protected and about our release. I talked and talked. The community hall was transformed into a dining hall and we indulged in an amazing feast. Every activity group in the church—the children, the youth, senior citizens—came to us at the front and hung garlands of flowers around our necks, Marianne, me, the children and Silke. They were piled so high around our necks that we could hardly see over the top. And then each of these groups brought us gifts. These were simple Christians some of whom were very poor. They could very well identify with our losses inflicted by the Taliban. Now they presented us with very practical things such as plates, cups and pots—everything we needed for our household in Kabul. I was very moved, especially because a few weeks earlier, on our arrival in Pakistan, I had lent an Afghan friend all our cash. Presumably it was a short-term emergency loan—but I never got the money back. We were financially broke, and now these dear Christians helped us to restock our home.

PLANS FOR KABUL

The time in Peshawar did the whole Taubmann family good. They were able to cement friendships and encourage their colleagues. The work would continue in Pakistan on a good footing, and so they set a date to leave for Kabul. Len Stitt was already there and enquiring impatiently, "When are you coming? I'm waiting for you. I need you." Georg rented a truck and they loaded up their things and the gifts from the Pakistani Christians, ready to go.

Udo Stolte: I had been back from Pakistan for a while and was sitting in my office when a call came from the Foreign Office. "Mr. Stolte, we have found out that Mr. Taubmann wants to return to Kabul," said the chief official. "But we know from our sources that the new Supreme Court Judge Shinwari intends to resume the trial if the Shelter Now people return. Mr. Stolte, what shall we do? I request you urgently to exert your influence on him to change his mind. Please, hold him back!"

"Yes, I'll do what you say. I shall speak to him," I replied. "But I can already tell you his response. He won't listen to me."

During the phone call our pastor entered the office and heard what was going on. We decided to speak to Georg together.

Georg Taubmann: We were busily packing when a call came from Udo Stolte and the pastor of my church in Braunschweig. "Georg, we have just had a call from the Foreign Ministry in Berlin. News has been leaked to them that the new Supreme Judge has stated that the eight development workers will appear before the courts should they ever return to Afghanistan. "Please, Georg," my pastor urged, "consider the danger of the situation and stay where you are. It would be unthinkable if you were to be arrested again." He was probably envisaging the whole stress and media scrum which the congregation in Braunschweig would have to face.

But we were sitting on packed luggage and Len was urgently awaiting our support. "I well understand your concerns," I replied. "Please give us a day to think about it. We'll pray and chat about it." I took the warning very seriously. The very thought of being locked up again was unbearable. We prayed as a small team and the unbelievable happened: against every expectation and in spite of legitimate fears, we all had a deep peace and certainty: "Go, God is with you!"

At the same time we had to inform Len that we would have to delay our arrival in Kabul. He responded, "If you can't come, then I'm coming back. I cannot cope on my own." I knew even more clearly then, that if we didn't leave now, there would not in the foreseeable future, or perhaps ever, be a reconstruction of Shelter Now projects in Afghanistan.

> **Supreme Judge Faisal Ahmad Shinwari**
>
> When the new Afghan transition government was formed, the different parties, or rather people groups, who had fought against the Taliban, were given posts in the government. The Northern Alliance who represented the largest group, were given the most posts, for example, Defense, Foreign Affairs and the Interior Ministry. An Islamic conservative group claimed the Justice Ministry. They appointed Shinwari, a controversial character with radical Islamic views, as Supreme Judge. Among other things he supported the reintroduction of sharia, the banning of television and the restriction of women—as had been the case during the Taliban period.
>
> When questioned by a journalist about religious freedom in the new Afghanistan, Shinwari replied that he intended to reintroduce sharia, according to which there would be no religious freedom and attempts to do missionary work would be punished. In this context, he mentioned that if the freed development workers were to return, they would again be brought before the courts, because it had not been possible to complete outstanding law processes due to their absence.
>
> It was a monstrous statement. Just imagine that an innocent man, condemned by the Nazis, who had been able to escape before the collapse of the regime, were to be arrested again by a judge in the newly created post-war Federal Republic of Germany, and brought before the courts to continue the interrupted Nazi trial. This is how this judge wanted to proceed with the Shelter Now aid workers, although it had been proven that they had been held captive as hostages by the Taliban. A crazy proposal.

LOOKING BACK: BEFORE THE SUPREME COURT

This was an unveiled threat to the Shelter Now aid workers, which Shinwari, the Supreme Judge of the new transition government stated in the interview. If the freed aid workers returned, they would be brought to trial by him, because the outstanding court proceedings could not be completed by reason of their flight.

What had gone on before the Supreme Court six months earlier, after days imprisonment by the Taliban regime? How had the trial proceeded? What accusations were brought?

Condemned under Sharia
Day 37: September 8, 2001
Excerpt from the book Escape from Kabul

"Out, out, and be quick! You're going somewhere!"

A Taliban guard stormed into Georg Taubmann and Peter Bunch's cell and forced them outside. It was Saturday, September 8, about 10 o'clock and the pair were sitting together as usual and talking.

"What's up? Where are we going?" Peter wanted to know. He received no information, only "Hurry up! Hurry up!"

That was the nerve-wracking practice of the Taliban: to use rush and pressure to encourage premonitions of evil. Georg didn't even have time to comb his hair, much less to change his crumpled salwar kameez. He was just able to pull on a waistcoat as he went.

When they entered the inside courtyard a crowd of Taliban were already standing around a minibus. Shortly afterwards, the women were also led in. Surprised, the men and women looked at each other. What did the Taliban intend to do with them?

They had to get into the vehicle together and off they went. Ahead of them, they were preceded by the head of the prison in a jeep. An open pickup truck with at least six armed Taliban followed behind. Heavily guarded, they proceeded through the city.

"Where are they taking us?" the others asked Georg.

"No idea!" Georg tried hard to peer out of the bus window to try and orient himself as the surroundings glided past. In the minibus there were mixed emotions: uncertainty, creeping panic and curiosity. This was thinly overlaid with the pleasure of seeing something of the environment and of finally being together again. They exchanged news and found out how each individual was doing.

It was nice to get out of the narrow confines of their cells and to see life on the streets of Kabul. The prisoners knew the area well as the vehicle was going in the direction of Wazir Akbar Khan, the suburb where almost all of the Shelter Now staff lived. Georg was even able to look down his street in passing and recognize his house in the distance. Then at a large roundabout on the main road the vehicles turned off in the direction of the airport.

"Are they maybe taking us to the airport and just letting us go?" Georg had the sudden happy thought.

He didn't know that on this road immediately on the right was the Afghan Supreme Court. The convoy slowed down, stopped at the edge of the road and the Shelter Now colleagues stared at a huge group of reporters and cameramen, light bulbs flashing and film cameras whirring. They didn't know what was happening.

Bewildered and rather nervous, they got out. They were immediately led up steps into the lobby of the courtroom. Only now did the last of them realize that they were in the Supreme Court, where the really important cases and the most serious crimes were heard.

Margrit Stebner: The Taliban who had interrogated us up till now had never given any indication that we would be brought to trial. Indeed they encouraged us to hope that we would soon be freed or expelled from the country. Only Dayna's mother, during her visits, hinted that it might eventually come to trial.

When the guards loaded us into the vehicle that morning we had no idea where we were going. The sight of the Court building certainly was a shock for us; and we were also amazed at the presence of the press.

The Shelter Now aid workers had to wait 20 to 30 minutes in the lobby before they were admitted to the hearing. A female guard was present with them to watch for the women's "honor." As she had no command of English, the men and women spoke to each other unhindered. It was the first opportunity for them to hear from one another what they had been accused of in their interrogations.

They were also able to expose the misrepresentations and lies that the Taliban had told them individually.

For example, Georg had been told by the Taliban that Heather and Dayna had confessed that they had converted to Christianity the Afghan women to whom they had shown the film. Now he discovered that that was not at all the case.

Again, the women had been told that Georg had dismissed Katrin in a rage and replaced her with someone else. In addition, they said, he had made all sorts of confessions, for example that they kept piles of Bibles, Christian videos and CDs in the Afghan language concealed in their homes and offices. Georg had even supposedly apologized to the Taliban for engaging in missionary work.

But these had all been lies, designed to play them off against one another and to persuade them to make false confessions.

"Yes, we did show the Afghan family the documentary about Jesus," Dayna recounted. "But I had a funny feeling about it, because the Afghan women were really forcing us to. And I can now better understand why the boy almost shamefacedly demanded the book."

"During the interrogations we wanted to protect the Afghan family and explained that we had visited them on our own initiative," added Heather. "I suspect they were forced to invite us. We confessed to having spoken about religious topics, as is usual everywhere. But that's all."

Similarly, with Katrin, it was a case of the film and the children's project, which supposedly had been run illegally. She too had put up a brave fight during the interrogations.

There had been nothing of which to accuse the other four—Peter, Diana, Margrit and Silke. However, other things were misrepresented, like cooperating on the children's project, forbidden literature and the possession of radio cards. As none of it was true, they had signed nothing which could in any way incriminate them. There wasn't much the court could accuse them of. So they were curious as to what could be in store.

At last they were led into the courtroom. It was smaller than they expected—and packed full with lots of people. The accused had to sit in the front row. Behind them sat diplomats, who had heard of the court hearing only at the last minute and that more by chance. It had been they who had informed the world press. The remainder of the room was occupied by countless reporters who, although allowed to be present, were not permitted to take any photographs.

*The Shelter Now aid workers before the Supreme Court.
Drawing by Silke Dürrkopf*

Silke Dürrkopf: I had a good look at the room and at the people. At the front at the top end there was a massive writing desk on which the "wise" books were piled up. On the wall behind it hung a large framed picture with Koranic sayings. To the right and left, swords were attached to the wall. There was also a leather whip which the religious police always carried. The whip had a short handle to which a leather-covered steel cable was attached.

The presiding judge Nur Mohammed Sakib, wearing a white turban and black waistcoat, sat with a chilly countenance on a massive chair behind this desk. Up to 20 judges sat in a row to his right and his left, all with very large turbans and long beards. Most of them were very old, with extremely serious faces which I found very threatening. To the left beside the writing desk two more men squatted on the floor, writing down everything that was said. It was like a scene from a medieval film. To the right beside the table stood the translator, who tried hard to translate the judge's speech, during which much help had to be given by the public.

The language in the courtroom was Pashtu, which Georg Taubmann knew and was thus able to understand a good part of the speech. Furthermore, not much could be expected of the translator, partly because Nur Mohammed Sakib spoke in extremely long sentences, so that the English translation resulted in a sketchy summary.

The judge's speech was essentially a hymn of praise for sharia, the Islamic divine law from the Middle Ages. He emphasized that the punishment for their "crimes" would be according to Islamic law, the sharia, which could mean imprisonment as well as a fine, or even execution. Currently Taliban judges were in the process of studying Islamic law as it applied to the present case; they would administer a just punishment. However the Supreme Leader of the Faithful Mullah Mohammed Omar had the final word. The accused had the "full right" to defend themselves and also to appoint a lawyer of their choice.

Judge Nur Mohammed Sakib said, literally, "Sharia Law is full of mercy and justice." Later, after the Shelter Now colleagues had processed their shock, they laughed ironically at this statement.

Following on from this speech the accused and the diplomats were allowed to speak. Georg Taubmann used the opportunity to speak out before the judge and the world press. "For three weeks we have been undergoing interrogation. Up till now no one has told us what we are accused of and why we have been imprisoned. What crime have we committed?" he complained. "Four of our colleagues have absolutely nothing to do with this case and are sitting in custody, innocent. Why have we not been allowed contact with the outside world? Up to now we haven't even been able to speak to our families."

The judge did not deign to look at Georg Taubmann during his impassioned speech and made no response.

Georg continued with his speech. "You said we could take a lawyer of our choice, but how were we to do that when we knew nothing at all of this court sitting and were not allowed to speak to our diplomats?" Then the German diplomat Helmut Landes rose and demanded better access to the accused, in order to assist them in preparation of their defense.

The presiding judge adjourned the hearing. The High Court would have to investigate the accusations further, but he advised the authorities to facilitate the search for lawyers. A new date for a trial would be notified only after a lawyer had been found and the investigations complete.

The accused were immediately led outside and loaded into the waiting minibus. It all went so quickly that the reporters could scarcely take photographs, much less ask questions of the prisoners.

Georg Taubmann: The following day was my father's birthday. I had a great urge to send him my greetings on that day, to explain to him that I was well, and that he shouldn't worry about me. I was tormented that my parents knew absolutely nothing about me. How were they managing to deal emotionally with my being in custody? That must all have been awful for them.

We are a large family, I have seven brothers and sisters and we have a wonderful relationship. So a birthday is always an important occasion for us. It was immaterial where I was in the world, I always called my father. And now I could neither write to nor telephone him.

But all the press folk were standing in front of our minibus. So I quickly opened the window, leaned out, waved to them and shouted, "Please inform our par-

Georg Taubmann takes the opportunity to tell the press that the prisoners are fine

ents that they shouldn't worry. We are fine." And then I smiled deliberately into the whirring cameras, thinking of my father. The guards weren't pleased about this brief protest, but it was too late to prevent it.

The group was brought back to the prison under heavy guard. They squatted in the minibus with mixed feelings and first needed to process the past few hours. The attendance of reporters and cameramen had confused them. They had not known that they were in the forefront of world publicity. Was that to be regarded in a positive light? Would the world now fight more strongly for their release?

What was written about them in the newspapers? Or was the whole theater just a part of a Taliban show trial, by which the regime moved into the foreground of public interest and Christianity was defamed?

It troubled them deeply that the Supreme Court had been brought in, and that they were to be condemned according to Islamic law. That the death penalty was being considered had completely shocked them. They hadn't reckoned on such harshness.

The presiding judge was not unknown to Georg. As a close confidant of Mullah Mohammed Omar, Nur Mohammed Sakib was a feared man. He was a hardliner. Due to the many death sentences he had imposed he was constantly surrounded by bodyguards. No mercy was to be expected from Nur Mohammed Sakib!

In this precarious situation they definitely needed a lawyer, if possible one who knew all about sharia law. There was no longer any doubt about it. The whole procedure would certainly take up a lot of time. No thoughts now about an early release.

The outlook was depressing!

Two days later the diplomats were allowed to visit the Shelter Now aid workers, to advise them on the choice of lawyer. A judge and a representative of the Afghan Foreign Ministry were present during the discussion. The diplomats suggested the Pakistani advocate Atif Ali Khan from Peshawar. Although still quite young, he had studied sharia law among other things and would certainly be able to represent them well. The colleagues agreed.

It was to be another two weeks, however, until the prisoners were able to meet him for the first time, because one day later, September 11, an event occurred which not only shattered New York and the whole of the Western world, but also dramatically elevated the danger of the situation of the eight colleagues in custody.

Day 40: September 11, 2001

Georg Taubmann: I was sitting in our cell reading, when the door burst open and two friendly Taliban guards rushed in excitedly. "Mr. George, we have just heard on the radio that two airplanes have flown into the World Trade Center. Both towers have collapsed, there are supposed to be thousands dead. They say it's a terror attack and Osama bin Laden is behind it."

The two Taliban seemed really shattered; they were taking a great risk by telling me this. In the past weeks I had won over some of the guards as friends, who kept me up to date with the news and even smuggled some letters between the women and us. But it was becoming increasingly dangerous for them, as their colleagues who were loyal to the party line eyed them suspiciously. Among the latter, of course, there was great jubilation that they had got one over on the hated Americans. They celebrated their hero Osama bin Laden and were proud of him.

A sort of horror film ran before my eyes. It was immediately clear to me what this terror attack could mean for us prisoners and what would happen next.

Osama bin Laden was a close friend of Mullah Omar's; he was in Afghanistan, where his Al Qaeda fighters were trained and fought on the side of the Taliban. The USA would demand the extradition of Osama bin Laden. Mullah Omar would refuse, whereupon the Americans would react with military reprisals. All foreigners would leave Afghanistan, including our diplomats. We would remain as the only foreigners and in future be hostages in the hands of the Taliban. If attacked they could easily use us as human shields. In any case, from now on we were at the mercy of the Taliban's rage against foreigners.

This thought shook me to the core. In the previous 17 years I had experienced the furious anger of extreme Muslims and their aggression against foreigners several times. One can hardly forget the sight of fanatical mobs raging through the streets, looting and issuing threats. I was sure that after September 11, the world would never be the same again. And we Shelter Now people were in the eye of the storm.

On September 13, most foreigners left Afghanistan: the UN staff, employees of other foreign NGOs, foreign businessmen and experts, the diplomats of those who were imprisoned, as well as Heather Mercer's father and Dayna Curry's mother. Within the next few days the remaining foreigners followed.

Georg Taubmann and Peter Bunch recognized the sounds of the small Red Cross planes and those of the aid organization PACTEC which had foreigners on board—they had flown in them often enough. They heard them flying in and out of Kabul again and again.

Now we've been abandoned by everyone, thought Georg in disappointment. *Now only God can stand by us!*

Insecurity and anxiety spread among the Taliban. They were all sure that the Americans would do something to retaliate. Georg heard from the guards who were friendly to him that the USA was on the point of building up a worldwide alliance against terrorism. There was no doubt that international interest was focused on Afghanistan. Georg learned that Pakistan had sided with America and that the first aircraft carriers were already on their way.

The prisoners began to experience more evidence of the dreaded hatred of foreigners from some of the guards. This hatred showed itself in much stricter surveillance and threats, as if they were the authors of their own misfortune.

There's something quite dangerous brewing here. I hope nothing untoward happens, Georg thought to himself.

Although it took some time till he had overcome all the obstacles, the Pakistani lawyer Atif Ali Khan found his way to the prisoners, in spite of the tense situation. He was accompanied by his colleague Najib. Najib was a Pashtun and came from the very same tribal region as the prison governor. This fact appeased the Taliban somewhat, as they weren't exactly pleased that their prisoners had actually acquired a lawyer, *and* one who intimated that he was well versed in sharia law. In addition, Najib had studied in a madrassa, in which their judge Nur Mohammed Sakib had taught for some time.

The Lawyer Atif Ali Khan began by listening to his clients. He was a deeply convinced Muslim and therefore full of prejudice toward his clients. No wonder, as up till now he had heard only bad things about them: they had supposedly given out loads of Christian literature and Bibles in Afghanistan and bribed people to become Christians through their aid projects.

When Georg initially took Atif Ali Khan aside and asked what kind of penalty he and the team should expect, he answered coolly, "From what I have heard I expect a prison term or even the death penalty." But sharia did embody the principle of mercy and he would intervene on their behalf with that in mind. For Georg this was shocking news, but he kept it to himself.

However the more the lawyer interacted with his clients and searched for evidence, the more astonished—indeed appalled—he became at how badly the foreigners had been treated by the Taliban. Still he believed the trial would be fair and that he could have his clients freed.

But not only did alarming pieces of news reach them in prison via their lawyer, he also managed also to bring letters, newspapers and foodstuff from the German Embassy and the Shelter Now team in Pakistan. In the parcels were woolen jackets, warm underwear, socks, blankets, cosmetics, chocolate and snacks.

This was naturally a special surprise and a cause for celebration.

Only now, after six weeks in custody, did the German workers receive their mail. This had been withheld from them by the prison governor.

Georg Taubmann: When Peter and I were back in our cell, I opened my letters with trembling hands. To see my children's handwriting, to read from Marianne that they were doing well—that moved me very deeply and at the same time brought the pain of our separation bubbling to the surface. It was good that at least Peter was with me. He hugged me, comforted me and prayed for me.

Among the things which the lawyer had brought with him was a thick envelope with a collection of international press articles from the past weeks, which reported particularly on our capture. When I studied these, I understood for the first time the dimensions of our arrest and the huge international interest in our case. I had not expected such a response.

However the way in which we were portrayed in some newspaper articles directly after our arrest—as a small group of fanatical Christians who had been recklessly doing missionary work in Afghanistan— did disappoint me deeply. We had not only ourselves to blame for our plight, but had also endangered other development agencies.

Why did journalists suddenly believe the exaggerations and lies of the Taliban so unreservedly? The supposed evidence in the press photographs—for example, a crucifix, an audio cassette and an English Bible—didn't come from us. And anyway, it was ridiculous to condemn someone to death for that reason.

Surely the journalists knew how the Taliban treated human rights and people of other faiths? They had robbed their women of every right, destroyed the historic Buddha statues and didn't care a fig about international protests. They wanted to drive the Hindus out of their land and compel them to wear yellow strips of cloth so that they could be recognized—a macabre parallel to Hitler's Nazi Germany when Jews were forced to wear the yellow Star of David. The Taliban didn't pressure only us, but had already created difficulties for other aid organizations and closed down projects on the pretext of insignificant "misdemeanors."

Why, I wondered, did so few reporters bother to refer to the success of our 18-year development work in Pakistan as well as in Afghanistan? Why did so few write about how we helped refugees in great danger and how highly we and our work were recognized? After all, we had been requested by high-up Taliban to work in different regions in Afghanistan. They had even placed land and houses at our disposal for our work, without cost. Many well-known aid organizations, various UN agencies (like UNDP, UNCHS and WFP) and the governments of other countries supported our projects with huge financial contributions, and so highly recognized our commitment.

Even if two colleagues from our organization, on the basis of a request from Afghan friends, had shown a *Jesus* film, that did not by a long way justify the destruction of our aid work and our captivity. We would have liked some more consideration and respect from representatives of the western press. I needed some time to process these newspaper reports!

Day 59: September 30, 2001

On September 30, exactly three weeks after the first hearing before the Supreme Court, the Shelter Now aid workers were taken again to the Law Courts. Of course, without warning and in great haste. Again they were not informed where they were going.

Georg Taubmann: What I found so awful this time, was that they took a detour. My assumption that we were going to the court was thereby shattered. They went along the main street directly to Ariana Chowk, the notorious square where many hangings had taken place. At each public hanging this square was overflowing with curious onlookers.

"They're not going to…?" It was like a dagger through my heart. I didn't mention my terrible dread to the team. I shrunk back and peered anxiously out of the front window. "If there's a huge crowd there, then I know what's going to happen!"

The square came into view. No crowds! I was unspeakably relieved. It was cruel, the way they played around with our emotions!

When the group eventually arrived at the Supreme Court, no large press presence awaited them. One sole reporter from the Arabic broadcaster Al Jazeera filmed them with a small video camera.

The hearing proceeded disappointingly for them. The enmity of the Taliban for foreigners was very apparent, as the threatened bombardment by the USA could begin at any moment.

First of all the Shelter Now workers had to formally certify their lawyer. They were interested to hear the charges, to know finally what their situation was. The address and the charges were read out in Dari. However there was no translator for the accused, and even the lawyer couldn't understand anything, because he spoke only Pashtu.

"We want an interpreter," Georg protested as representative of the group. "If we cannot understand anything, we cannot respond."

His objection was completely ignored. For the judge, it was obviously only a show trial.

"We require a copy of the charges in English," the lawyer chipped in.

This was provided, but not until four days later. Even then it was confusing and imprecise. Names were switched around and the English translation in parts was so bad that one could not work out the meaning.

The lawyer thereupon received from the Court a period of 15 days for his defense statement.

Margrit Stebner: The whole proceedings before the court were a joke. For example, for the formal certification of our lawyer, all our photographs were stuck into a thick book and each of us had to put a thumb print below our picture.

We couldn't follow the reading of the charges in Dari, and when we held the English translation in our hands four days later, we had the impression that the judge hadn't a clue who the four of us were—Peter, Diana, Silke and I—and so had confused us with one another. We read for the first time why we were charged and were outraged over the ridiculously minimal and invented accusations. We had sat for nine weeks in a miserable cell for that?

The lawyer, Atif Ali Khan, sat with the prisoners and went through the charges point by point, and each of them made their statement.

Most of the charges were twisted or invented. To take from the few personal objects left behind by a former colleague as evidence of proselytizing on the part of the aid organization was ridiculous. It was also untrue that no permission for the children's project existed. Dayna Curry had given the Afghan family neither a radio nor a radio card. To accuse Diana Thomas of possession of a radio card was false, for she had said exactly the opposite in her interrogation transcript.

Peter Bunch and Margrit Stebner had definitely not been involved in the children's project. To charge the two of them and Silke Dürrkopf made it clear it was obviously enough simply to have been employed in the aid organization.

Atif Ali Khan promised to work fast on the defense statement and then to hand it in to the court. In view of the pathetic charges, he was optimistic that they would soon be released.

The lawyer had also received a copy of a communication between Mullah Omar and the German Embassy in Islamabad, which dealt with mission work by foreigners. According to this communication, foreigners who had tried to convert Muslims to Christianity should be sentenced to up to ten days in prison and then expelled from the country, if the charge was proved. The Shelter Now aid workers had already been over two months in prison without any proof of the charge of converting Muslims. When the lawyer presented this clear ruling by Mullah Mohammed Omar to the judges, it was of minimal interest to them.

In all his work, every possible obstacle was placed in Atif Ali Khan's way. For example, the head of the prison refused him access to his clients. When the lawyer wished to complain about this at the Supreme Court, he was not permitted to meet the judges. Officials pretended not to be present. And they did not deal with important papers.

Finally, Atif Ali Khan left Kabul, irritated and in haste, supposedly to be able to work on the papers in peace in Peshawar. But it was more likely because he was afraid of the bombing which the Americans had already begun.

When the lawyer returned a week later, he presented his defense statement to the eight colleagues. Together they corrected and changed some points. When this work was finished, Atif Ali Khan went to the Supreme Court to hand in the statement, but there was no one to deliver it to. The presiding judge simply sent a message to him that the High Court had more important business to see to, than to be concerned with the accused.

Feeling extremely depressed, Atif Ali Khan returned to his clients in the prison. His carefully crafted defense statement had not even been acknowledged.

"Here it's not a matter of a just legal system," Georg Taubmann had said to him long before. "It doesn't matter what you set before the judges, they will do with us what they want. For them we are simply hostages. There's no point in waiting for the end of the trial. It's purely a waste of time. We've got to do something different!"

Now Atif Ali Khan believed him. "Georg, they are playing a dirty game with you here," he said, completely disillusioned. "We're stuck in a cul de sac. The only help we have now is massive pressure on the part of western countries!"

After that, he went back to Pakistan, defeated and disappointed, and never returned to Kabul. The Taliban forbade him any further contact with his clients.

A few days later all contact between the outside world and the prisoners was completely cut off. The international public no longer knew how they were or what was happening to them.

Back in Kabul

Despite Judge Shinwari's threat to bring the Shelter Now team to court should they return to Afghanistan, after a period of thinking about it, everyone on the team in Peshawar had an inner peace and the certainty a day later that it was right to go. So they loaded up the last of the luggage, and got into the cars— Georg, Marianne, the two boys, as well as Silke and an American colleague— and drove to Kabul. They arrived in early June 2002, a good six months after their rescue in Ghazni.

Len Stitt was very relieved to have reinforcements at last, and that Georg with his many years of experience took over leadership of the team, with Marianne's support. For Georg it was a huge challenge. His lingering burnout made it tough for him. He hadn't expected that confronting his old environment would be such a drain emotionally.

FLASHBACKS AND ECSTATIC JOY

Georg Taubmann: On the one hand I was absolutely delighted to be back in Kabul, on the other I was again encountering the places which caused me horror. Now I had to drive past them frequently. During my imprisonment I was locked up in five different prisons.

First of all, everything had to be rebuilt. There was nothing left. The old office had been looted, and the rent had risen so much in the meantime that we couldn't afford the same rooms. So we had to search for new office space and furnish it. Only now did we learn that our old office was directly opposite the plot of land where Osama bin Laden had lived. It was one of his houses where he stayed when he came to Kabul. Without knowing it, we had looked out of our office windows at the houses where he and his cohorts had lived.

Every day when I drove from our newly rented house to the office, I had to pass the prison where I was interrogated for weeks. Our new house was situated near this prison. If I looked out of our living room window, I caught sight of a hill with a strongly fortified house on the top. From the inner courtyard of the prison I had also seen the same building, but from the other side. When I looked at it, the same feelings arose as I had had in prison. Suddenly it was a trigger. Sometimes certain sounds and smells produced uncontrollable flashbacks and dreadful scenes would appear before my eyes which I simply could not eradicate. I just had to learn to deal with it.

We had a lot of guests too. People who visited us wanted, of course, to see the places where we had been held captive. I had said I'd be prepared to make a documentary of our imprisonment and release with an American film crew. Because of that we searched out all the prisons in which we'd been held and interrogated. We traveled the stretch of road leading to Ghazni and actually found the exact container in which we had spent a gruesome, cold night. These things stirred up my emotions dreadfully. On the other hand it was good that I allowed it, as I learned through time to handle it more and more, and the flashbacks decreased.

The greatest counterbalance to the negative feelings that kept being stirred up was the incredible freedom and lightheartedness I encountered on the streets of Kabul. Music pealed out of stores and crowds of people jostled laughingly with each other in the bazaars. Somehow we felt safe and that we belonged. Hardly any women were to be seen in burkas but instead with brightly colored headscarves. Wedding halls and businesses for arranging marriages were shooting up everywhere. The restaurants competed for customers and even offered alcoholic drinks. It seemed as if everyone wanted to make up for all they had missed. To me, it was slightly over the top. Life in the city of Kabul had completely changed.

Marianne Taubmann: It was the same for me as for Georg. We knew the period under Taliban rule, when there was so much oppression in the city of Kabul. To me it was like being under a lid without any life. Everywhere there were children and women begging. When we returned in the middle of 2002, it was a totally different city. People had music on in the shops, everywhere you could see pictures on the walls. One really saw and sensed an atmosphere of life and

> A few years later it all looked quite different again. The attacks increased and more and more people, especially foreigners, left the country. Where there had previously been freedom and hope, now oppression, hopelessness and fear returned. There were many barricades and security measures. Almost every day people were wounded or killed. The people scarcely dared to go to restaurants or attend big functions, because they are always afraid of becoming victims of an attack.

hope. One evening when we were going through the city, the people were dancing in the street. The difference between night and day! Previously there was oppression, hardship and depression. Then suddenly it was as if it had all blown away. The city was full of life and full of hope. There was lots of initiative. Houses were being built, streets repaired. Girls came streaming out of the schools in their uniforms—black coats and white headscarves. It wasn't like that before. The Taliban hadn't allowed girls' schools. Under the Taliban you could almost have counted off the restaurants on one hand and it was unpleasant to go out for a meal. Whenever Al Qaeda people came in, they scolded and threatened the guests. And now restaurants were shooting up like mushrooms.

Georg reported how he had to drive past places of terror again and again on his trips through Kabul. What caused him particular torment was the sight of the prisons where he had witnessed and experienced such dreadful things himself.

The first three weeks, Georg and his Australian colleague, Peter Bunch, had simply vegetated in a small cell in solitary confinement. They were neither allowed to receive mail nor to write letters. And they knew nothing of what was happening outside. In total he had spent his prison sentence in five different jails.

LOOKING BACK: REMEMBERING THE PERIOD OF CAPTIVITY

Excerpt from the book *Escape from Kabul*

Day 3: August 5, 2001

Georg Taubmann: On Sunday afternoon when the Taliban led us into the cell of the prison of the Religious Police, we were shocked at first. I had never been in a prison. I only knew about it from hearsay. We were locked in a small room measuring about 2.5 x 3 meters. There was neither chair nor cupboard, only two thin, filthy mattresses on the floor. We had no pillows, no blankets, only the clothes we wore. When we arrived, we squatted down on the floor and were speechless for a while. We sat there and simply couldn't take it in. The arrests had hit us like a hammer blow.

It was hot in the prison. The air was suffocating from the remains of food and hordes of flies buzzed around us.

After a while I got up and tried to orient myself in the semi-darkness. A bare bulb that gave out a pathetic light hung from the ceiling. On the side opposite the door there were windows, but they only showed the way to the kitchen where cooking was done for the Taliban. Hence the wretched kitchen odor and constant noise. In the cell there was another second smaller area which was hung with a strip of cloth. This was frequently drawn to the side and a curious Talib glared at us darkly.

The walls had holes, the floor was covered with filth. I got very afraid of the insects, as it was quite possible that there were snakes and scorpions. The mattresses were infested with bed bugs which attacked poor Peter very soon. From then on he had swellings over his whole body.

It is truly dreadful to be imprisoned. You sit or lie, walk a few paces up and down, and can do nothing. You can't even sleep properly with the endless noise from the kitchen and the constant surveillance.

And then my thoughts wandered over and over again to my team. Who all had been arrested? I knew about Heather and Dayna and some Afghan employees, but who else? How many of them? How were they doing

And what about my wife Marianne and my two boys? Had the Taliban searched our house? Were Marianne and the children also imprisoned? The worries were unbearable!

Good that Peter was with me, that I didn't have to be alone. That was a real comfort. Together we poured out our hearts to God, which sounded just like the Psalms of Lament in the Bible.

Day 4: August 6, 2001

The first night for the two men was brief. Georg dozed rather than slept in the strange environment. Peter had it easier. He could sleep well always and everywhere.

Shortly before 4 o'clock, the first Taliban shuffled past their cell to the toilet, to do his ceremonial washing. Then punctually at four the prayer call of the mullah rang out. Morning prayer followed, and the pair were kept awake by further religious singing from the madrassa. On top of that, the smells and the noise from the kitchen assailed them, and off and on, a Talib gawked at them through the window. At about 7 o'clock they got their breakfast—naan bread and green tea.

In the following days, Georg refused all food. The only thing he took was bottled water which he had a guard bring him from the bazaar. Fortunately he still had a little money on him for that.

"Mr. George, why are you not eating anything?" he was asked time and again.

In reply, Georg complained loudly each time. "This place is unfit for human habitation. Take us somewhere else. The stench from the kitchen, the heat, the noise, the darkness—it's unbearable! Why on earth are we here? We haven't committed any crime. Let us go!"

Obviously, he was complaining to the wrong people. For almost a week nothing changed in their miserable condition.

Day 8: August 10, 2001

For Georg Taubmann and Peter Bunch the early days in the prison of the Religious Police went by full of uncertainty, boredom and anxious questions, wondering how things might proceed.

Then, on Friday morning, there was suddenly a great hustle and bustle.

"Out, out! Get your things and come with us!" Georg was hastily called out of his cell. It was part of the Taliban tactics to confront prisoners with new situations unprepared.

Peter watched Georg go with irritation and had to remain behind on his own.

"Where are we going? Why can't Peter come too?" Georg asked with concern.

Without saying a word to him, the guards led Georg to his first interrogation, which would last from late afternoon till late into the night, in the re-education institute. That was where the six women were also held, although Georg was unaware of this at this point. The men didn't bother taking him back again.

Instead he was put into a cell there, was allowed to sleep a few hours, and the next morning the interrogation was continued.

The new cell, in which Georg had to spend the next three days alone between interrogation sessions, was just as small as the first, but slightly more comfortable. (Peter was eventually transferred there.) It wasn't quite so filthy, there was less noise and, best of all, no kitchen smells. But again only two thin mattresses on the floor, and not a piece of furniture. The cupboard at the wall belonged to the person on guard duty, who came in continually to fetch things out of it. The window was facing north, with a wall behind it, so they never got to see the sun. The door was unlocked so that they could freely go to the toilet, which was next door to their cell. However there was always a guard sitting on duty in the corridor outside.

The officials, four or five men in all, took turns interrogating. Two of them were clearly well trained in this activity. One of them, who was especially aggressive, was later dubbed "Long Nose" by the prisoners. Occasionally, when religious matters were being dealt with, the mullah from the adjoining madrassa came as well.

Due to the different languages and the complicated procedure the interrogations proceeded at a snail's pace. First the interpreter would write down the official's question in English. Then Georg answered in English, which was then translated orally into Pashtu. Following that, Georg himself had to write down his answer in English and sign it, with the date.

Georg Taubmann: The writing of my signature was the critical point for me! The questions demanded crazy concentration from me, because I had to watch what I answered, especially with repeat questions. With their accusations they constantly tried to squeeze false confessions out of me. After each question and answer session I was totally drained and exhausted. The longer an interrogation lasted—once for 16 hours straight—the more difficult it was for me to keep alert.

At the beginning, the officials made themselves out to be reasonably friendly, but their mood and their questioning technique could quickly switch. Some hearings were very aggressive and threatening. I was totally at their mercy. I certainly wasn't beaten, but I was often verbally abused to my wits' end.

Initially it was essentially about the aid organization. Which projects were we involved in? How many foreign workers did we have? How many Afghans were active? They wanted to know exactly where our houses were. How much advance rent we had paid? They even wanted to see our rental contract.

An especially critical topic was our children's project. The Taliban maintained that we were pursuing this project illegally and had secretly set up a madrassa, to instruct children in Christianity.

Of course, we had discussed the project with the Planning Authority and also received permission for it. Except now the employees in the Planning agency couldn't remember it because they were afraid of the religious police. The relevant paperwork had, interestingly enough, disappeared in the meantime.

"And how many teachers did you employ? What are their names? Where do they live?" they would enquire at every opportunity.

"We did not work illegally, for we had permission. We also had neither a madrassa nor teachers. We did not teach any children. We only shared out food and allowed them to do crafts for an hour a day, so that they could earn a little money," I repeatedly answered them.

"No, no, that is not correct! We have information that Christian instruction was given there. You as director must know that."

They were lying through their teeth and trying by any means to get a confession out of me.

A further charge was our supposed Christian proselytizing. The showing of the *Jesus* film was a welcome gift for them. The mullah from the madrassa was of course present at this hearing.

"As director you are responsible for everything," they shouted at me. "In our country it is a criminal offence to show such a film."

"I can't be held responsible for everything that my colleagues do in their free time," I answered. "Anyway, this film has already been shown publicly on television in many Muslim countries. In Pakistan many Muslims have watched it. Isn't Jesus a great prophet also with you?"

"But you have made Muslims in Afghanistan become Christians!" they shouted. "Afghans talk frequently about religion," I defended myself. "They ask us what we believe, and we answer that we are Christians. Is one not allowed to talk about religion in your country?" I asked in response.

"That may well be, but you use your relief organization as bribery and make the refugees in the camps become Christians by giving them money and goods!" they contradicted me.

"No, we do not! Shelter Now is a social relief organization, and we build houses, install bore wells and see that food aid is distributed fairly. We help everyone, regardless of their faith, and we do it without expecting anything in return.

"No, we have evidence against you! We found a host of Christian literature and Bibles in the women's house and in yours!"

"Then produce the evidence!" I knew very well that they couldn't prove it.

At that the Talib whom we called "Long Nose" became very loud and aggressive. He screamed, "You are criminals!"

I wasn't going to let this accusation go unchallenged. So I too became loud. "Isn't a criminal someone who has robbed or killed another person, but surely not someone who shows a Jesus documentary?" I replied. "Just go to our camps, where we have been providing your Afghan refugees with food for years. Look at the camps in Pakistan! Ask the Afghans who know us in Kandahar, in Helmand,

Khost and Logar and have seen our projects. Go there and ask the people there what they have to say about us. They respect us and are deeply grateful for all that we have done to help them. It's a huge insult and deeply wounding for me to be called a criminal."

At that they ended the questioning in silent embarrassment.

For two weeks they went on interrogating me like this. It was a very hard time for me. I asked Peter to pray for me during my interrogations. As soon as I'd hear footsteps in the corridor coming in our direction, I would sometimes flinch and fear would overwhelm me. "Here we go again with these dreadful interrogations!"

The time behind prison walls dragged on. The hope of an early release disappeared more and more. It gave way to the anxious question "What sort of game are they playing here?"

Day 46: September 17, 2001

On September 17, a good week after the first hearing before the Supreme Court, the men and women from Shelter Now were unexpectedly transferred to another place. For the men it was the third prison, for the women the second.

A guard stormed into their cell and barked, "Get moving! Pack your stuff! You're going to another place. The vehicle's waiting!"

"What's the meaning of this?" Georg resisted. "Who gave the order? We're not going. We're staying here!"

"No! That's a command!"

The two men, however, offered such strong resistance that the prison governor had to come personally and order them: "You must go! You have no other choice. We're taking you to a better place outside Kabul, which is also safer and nicer."

Maybe they're putting us under house arrest and we can have a more pleasant life, they both hoped on the basis of this information. So they packed their few things together and got into the vehicle beside the women, who were already there.

Again they were closely guarded during the journey, as a pick-up truck full of heavily armed Taliban followed their minibus. All eight of them were surprised and somewhat disturbed at this sudden transfer. Nevertheless, they used the opportunity of being together to tell each other the latest news. Meanwhile Georg was carefully watching the streets they were going along. He knew the roads well, as their administrative offices were in this part of the city.

To their consternation the whole journey took only ten minutes. The minibus then stopped in front of a large archway in the area of Shar-e Naw. Georg knew this archway well, as he had often passed it previously on his errands; a Taliban guard was always sitting in front of it. At that time he always used to wonder what was hidden behind this archway. Now they were going through it. After about 50 meters they passed another gate and found themselves in a prison yard surrounded by high walls and barbed wire.

The aid workers immediately protested. "You wanted to take us out of the city to a nicer, safer place! This is another prison!"

"This is your new accommodation. This is where you'll stay. Get out of the bus!" was the abrupt answer.

Yet again the Shelter Now team had been deceived and lied to. So, of course, it was absolutely not a safe place, especially in view of the expected bombardment by the American forces.

The women were shoved so quickly through a side door into their prison wing that Georg and Peter scarcely had time to say goodbye.

On their arrival Peter Bunch and Georg Taubmann were led into a courtyard which was part of the men's prison. This was an old, crumbling building with barred windows. Lots of prisoners were standing around in the yard and looked at them partly with curiosity, partly with apathy. For both men, their first impressions of this place were terrible. Carrying their luggage, a blanket and a plastic bag as their only possessions, they were led through the entrance, a large rusty iron door. In the building it was quite dark, so that they could make out hardly anything as they went up a sort of concrete stairway to the upper floor.

Once there, they went through a second door with a grille and along a dark corridor. On the right and left were cells with doors that were covered on both sides with sheets of steel and with a small peephole at eye level. The doors were lying open and the prisoners were lounging around in the hallway. They gave the impression of being intimidated, fearful and depressed. When the two foreigners appeared, however, they watched them walk by with amazement and curiosity.

The cell which was allocated to Peter and Georg was 2 x 3 meter in size. The window was quite large and barred. It provided a view over a yard at the back and showed that the building was designed in an L shape. Once again the room was extremely dirty, and the walls were covered with the scribbled names and dates of previous inmates. On the left side of the cell was a filthy steel shelf and beside the right wall stood a single rickety iron bed with an incredibly filthy mattress.

Georg Taubmann: Peter and I sat down on an old bed with a simple steel frame; we were shattered. We first needed to process all this. Again we had been deceived and lied to, for—instead of being in a nice house—we had now landed in the secret service prison.

The Afghan prisoners stood silently in the doorway and gawked at us. "What are these foreigners doing here?" they were probably asking each other. Somehow they noticed that we were in a state of shock, as, after a short time, one of them addressed me in Pashtu, asking if he could help us in any way. He was quite astonished and delighted that I knew his language. These pathetic figures immediately came alive and bombarded us with questions.

I asked, "Would there be a second bed anywhere for us?"

Within moments some of them went off to try and find one. The others set about helping us to clear up and clean the cell. It didn't take long for our fellow prisoners to rustle up a second old iron bed for us, and together we tried to maneuver it into the small cell. It worked, but unfortunately we were left with only a tiny space of less than a meter between both beds. I didn't even want to touch the mattresses and the pillows were full of holes and vermin. Fortunately

The appalling sanitary conditions in Kabul prison

we had some money that we were able to give to one of the prison guards to buy a powder that we used to get rid of the vermin. Then I spread out my second salwar kameez as a sheet on the bed and my second handkerchief on the pillow, a handkerchief I had received from the diplomats.

After the "renovation work" had been completed on our cell, I did a round of our floor to get to know our surroundings. What I discovered was a further culture shock. The rotten wooden doors on the toilets had fallen out of their frames and a curtain full of holes had to suffice. Behind it was hidden a platform with three holes which were full to overflowing with excrement. No one bothered to see that this was ever cleaned. The stench was so overpowering that I nearly vomited.

During my tour I discovered that there were about 50 prisoners in this wing who were permitted to move about freely in the corridor. Only the exit had grilles and was under guard. In the afternoons the prisoners were allowed to go out into the open air in the prison yard. After the six weeks of isolation, when I was only allowed right at the end to go outside briefly a few times, it was a great relief to be able to move my legs. The unrestricted interaction with fellow prisoners was also new for me. A new chapter in the everyday life of prison opened up. Up till now I had only had contact with the Taliban guards, but now, through the stories of the imprisoned men, I got to learn about a world of everyday Afghan life, a world which had hitherto been closed to me.

In the previous 17 years, I had got to know Afghans from every level of society. I had chatted with rich Afghans in their opulent homes in Peshawar and

Kabul. I had been a guest at extravagant weddings, and had dined with influential men in grand hotels.

On the other hand I had also spent a lot of time with Afghan refugees in the camps we had erected, and provided them with water and food. I had listened to their tales of suffering and their odyssey through Afghanistan. Many had had to flee before the Taliban, others had had to abandon their homes and fields, because after years of drought they could no longer support their families. In remote Afghan villages I had sat with the various tribal chiefs, including leaders of the mujahideen. Several of them were adventurous types who boasted of their gigantic arsenals of weapons. I had stayed overnight in the *hudjaras*, the Pashtuns' guesthouses, and drunk tea in the tents of nomads wandering in the Steppes.

So I knew life in the city and life on the land; I knew how the rich and the poor lived. But the life of Afghans such as I encountered here in the prison was totally foreign to me. I had, of course, heard about it, but I had no idea that the suffering was so immense. Here behind the prison walls, I discovered that almost every family in Afghanistan had suffered endlessly after the king was ousted in a revolt in 1973. They had lost their property, were driven out, arrested, tortured and shot or hanged. Since 1979, the beginning of the Soviet invasion, almost every family in Afghanistan had mourned the death of loved ones.

I got to know a dimension of life of the Afghan people which shocked me to the core, and for that reason deepened my love for them. It was worth the deprivations in this hideous prison to gain this authentic insight. I could never have gotten it anywhere else.

From the first day, I became friends with these men. They had all experienced a unique and tragic history. They came into our

Georg and one of his fellow prisoners

cell, squatted on our mattresses and on the floor, and we talked with one another about our lives, sometimes late into the night.

I tried to help my Afghan fellow inmates whenever I could. I encouraged them and supplied them with medicine. I borrowed money from Silke, who had smuggled more money into the prison than the rest of us, so that I could slip them something for themselves and their starving relatives.

Unfortunately, this sitting together and chatting with the prisoners in Georg and Peter's cell was not tolerated for long. The prison leaders became suspicious and introduced spies into the group to gather information. Eventually, they forbade the Afghan prisoners from frequent contact with the foreigners. Georg therefore changed tactics. He would stroll through the different cells every now and then, and chat with this one and that one, and so became the friend of nearly all the prisoners.

A minority of imprisoned Afghans in this prison were members of the Pashtun tribe; the majority were Tajiks, Uzbeks, Hazara or followers of the Northern Alliance leader Massood, assassinated just before the attack on the World Trade Center by Al Qaeda. There were both old and young men from all over Afghanistan, imprisoned merely because they belonged to the "wrong" people group or had been accused of having worked for opposition parties.

Among them, for example, was a group of honorable old men with white beards, who had done nothing wrong, but simply weren't on the same wavelength as the Taliban. And there was a group of simple nomads, called *Kuchi*, who had been traveling through the area with their camels and sheep and were not remotely interested in politics. They were simply accused of being loyal to the king and had been imprisoned. Georg chatted with them and found out that they didn't even know the name of the deposed king. Fortunately their tribe was able to pay a huge bribe and they were soon set free.

One of the prisoners had had a stationery shop, in which the henchmen of the religious police had found postcards with pictures of Indian actresses. As a result he was imprisoned for six months.

A particular target of the Taliban were the men who supported Massood, the murdered leader of the Northern Alliance. Anyone who was suspected of sympathizing with him was arrested and put in this secret service prison.

Sometimes the mere comment of an ill-disposed neighbor was sufficient grounds for an arrest. Most men who came under such suspicion remained six months to a year in this prison, then were then shunted off to other prisons where they had to serve the remainder of their sentence.

It was particularly distressing that there were no lawyers to represent these men. The relatives could only go to the "judge" and negotiate directly with him. But then it was always only about a bribe. The sums demanded were so absurdly high that many could not pay. One prisoner told Georg that his family was about to sell their house in order to secure his freedom. From then on the whole family would have to live in a refugee camp.

Many prisoners reported that they were the only breadwinners for their family and mostly for other relatives as well. Frequently, there were sisters-in-law and sisters with their children who belonged to the family, since their husbands having been killed in the war. So they were dependent on a man now in prison to provide for them. The previous year Kabul had over 10,000 widows. And now these men were sitting in prison; there were no male relatives left who could earn money. No wonder that many families sold all their possessions in order to survive. And those who had nothing more to sell had to starve.

The men who sat with Georg and told their life stories reported unanimously that had all been severely beaten upon their arrest. They spoke of the "cables"— steel cables approximately as thick as one's middle finger and covered with a layer of plastic.

"I got 100 cables when I was arrested," one said. And another reported, "Every day I got 50 cables." Still others reckoned their torture in periods of time: "I got cables for two hours."

In the course of their imprisonment, Georg Taubmann and Peter Bunch often heard the swish of the blows and the cries of the men from the torture chamber. Holding their ears didn't help. While they were forced to listen to these merciless tortures, Georg and Peter sat as if petrified, and could do nothing other than pray, "Lord, have mercy on them...."

Georg Taubmann and Peter Bunch in their cell

Georg Taubmann: During our daily afternoon outings in the prison yard, on several days in succession I saw a man lying on the grass writhing in pain. Eventually I went over to him. I assumed he was ill and had a temperature or diarrhea. But I heard from him that he was beaten every day. He showed me his wounds and complained of severe pain, so I gave him the highest dose of painkillers that I could find.

The story of another prisoner, an engineer, pursued me in my dreams. I had noticed him immediately because of his helpfulness and friendly manner, and he became a real friend during our internment. He had been arrested by the Taliban because a neighbor had slandered him.

Before that, he had been locked up for seven years in the notorious Pul-e-Charki prison, three years of which he had spent chained up in an underground dungeon. He wasn't able to cut his hair or his fingernails and had to answer the call of nature right where he was.

During this time his relatives had no idea where he was, which was why they assumed him to be dead. He told me of his loneliness and despair during these years, especially because no one came to visit him. His fellow prisoners in the meantime had either been released or hanged, whereas he just vegetated in his chains. When he finally was released, he was mentally disturbed. He had wandered through the streets and was unable to find his home. For a while, he spent nights in a mosque.

When he did finally find his house, his family was completely appalled at his appearance and the state he was in. It was only then that he found out that his father and his brother had died. His young wife was so traumatized by his appearance that she too died of the shock a month later.

I could tell many more tragic stories. An engineer who had experienced so much suffering was an unusually humble and helpful man. In general, I discovered that many of those who had experienced the most terrible things that one could ever imagine, were quite extraordinary characters. Their sympathetic and helpful bearing struck me and the way they could rejoice over the most trivial little thing. They were different from the Afghans I knew "outside."

Of course, among those who had suffered much there were also those who remained mentally confused or sought refuge in drugs. But I got to love them, chatted with them and helped them as far as I could with my limited means.

In general there was surprisingly little tension among the prisoners. Relationships were different from what one might imagine or how they are portrayed in films.

Occasionally there would be verbal arguments between the different tribal groups, but no violent conflicts. And, of course, there was tension after the prison leadership had bribed some prisoners to spy on our conversations and friendships. It really hurt me that, of all people, one of my fellow prisoners whom I had often supported and helped out with medication, betrayed us to the prison authorities, right down to the smallest detail.

A short time after Peter Bunch and Georg Taubmann had been delivered into the secret service prison, a group of students was taken into custody. The Taliban had arrested them under the accusation of belonging to the Massood sympathizers of the Northern Alliance. Among them was Mohammed Sharif, a Pashtun who spoke very good English. He came from an area in Afghanistan where the Shelter

Now relief agency had erected a factory for making prefabricated concrete slabs for houses. So Georg had often been in Mohammed Sharif's hometown and knew many of his people.

Before his own arrest Mohammed Sharif had heard on Radio Sharia that some foreigners had been arrested for apparently spreading Christianity. His tribe immediately suspected that this referred to the Shelter Now people and that it was just a Taliban accusation. Now he was in the same prison and was eager to get to know the highly respected Mr. George.

The two men quickly formed a close relationship and spent lots of time together. As Mohammed Sharif knew English well, it was possible for Peter to follow their conversations as well, as otherwise Georg spoke mainly in Pashtu with the other prisoners.

The three of them often ate their lunch and evening meals together, because Mohammed Sharif had a certain privileged position in the prison, since he came from a well known and powerful tribal group. The prison governor Mullah Hassan knew that he would have trouble with the tribe if he ever oppressed Mohammed as he did the other prisoners. Mohammed was therefore able to be with Georg as often as he wished. As well, he didn't have to participate in the usual prison duties and could even move about freely in the prison office. This meant that he had the chance to hear the news on radio and to listen in on Taliban conversations.

Mohammed cared for Georg and Peter very touchingly and intervened on their behalf with the prison administration. He saw to it that they could visit the women's prison every day and that they were never maligned as foreigners.

Mohammed Sharif was amazed how well Georg knew his homeland and his customs. So he wanted to know everything there was to know about Georg's life and how Georg's aid organization had helped his fellow countrymen. Because they had so much time, they sat together for hours and talked and talked.

Mohammed Sharif and also the other prisoners were deeply impressed at the way Peter Bunch and Georg Taubmann practiced their faith. As there was a constant coming and going between the cells, their fellow prisoners often came by in the morning when Peter and Georg were having their prayer time and reading the Bible.

"Can you please leave us alone for a while? We're just praying," Georg would usually request of them.

But the other prisoners would nevertheless stand in the doorway and wait for some minutes. For them, prayer was a ritual which only took a few minutes. But to their astonishment, these foreigners went on and on, praying and reading their Holy Book for a long time! And since Georg fasted every Friday, their holy day, he rose even more in their estimation!

"You are real believers," they said admiringly, "not like so many foreigners who don't believe in God and don't possess a Holy Book."

Sometimes they came and simply wanted to look at Georg's Bible. After all, holy books were well known to them, as Islam recognizes four Holy Books—the Koran, the Tawrat and the Zabur (the five books of Moses and the Psalms), and the Injil (the New Testament). But many of them had never seen an Injil and requested to hold it in their hands. Before they did this, however, they first washed their hands, then took it respectfully and pressed it to their hearts. Some even kissed the Bible with great reverence.

Several prisoners asked Georg to read from it. They were curious and inquisitive, although they had learned from their mullahs that the Christians' holy book was a forgery. The subject of "faith" remained a current topic. They held long discussions about it and the Afghans often left the room afterwards deep in thought. "How can these foreigners, who respect our Muslim faith, are themselves so devout and have helped many Afghan refugees, how can they be locked up here?" was a question asked by many of their fellow inmates.

The great openness of Georg Taubmann towards the Afghans and the clear evidence of his friendship won the Shelter Now aid workers much respect from among the prisoners as well as from most of the Taliban guards. The attacks of the hardliners and the guards who hated foreigners in general were thereby minimized. Who knows what would have happened to them, if they hadn't been so knowledgeable about the culture and conducted themselves so wisely?

The day for the release of the Afghan students came more quickly than anyone had anticipated. Normally, as soon as the prisoners heard of their release, they were so overjoyed they disappeared without much of a farewell. But Mohammed Sharif didn't look at all happy. When he received the good news, he went straight to Georg Taubmann. "I got the communication about my release," he said. "But I'm not going. I'm staying with you until you're released. I've spoken to my father and grandfather and they agree, even though they'd obviously like to have me back."

That was mid-October and Mohammed Sharif could not have guessed that it would be a further four weeks before the Shelter Now development workers would be set free. This decision was moreover extremely courageous of him, considering that the situation in Kabul had become very dangerous because of the increasing bomb attacks by the US fighter aircraft, and the battles which were being waged between Taliban fighters and the Northern Alliance only 30 kilometers away on the frontline to the North.

Georg and Peter were very touched by this honorable and friendly gesture, a gesture which also deeply impressed their fellow prisoners.

One day the other prisoners said, "Mr. George, we have found out that your 16 Afghan employees are also imprisoned here. In two cells, one leads to the inner courtyard, the other out to the back."

As a rule it was privileged prisoners who kept watch inside the individual cell wings. Georg had been able to win over one of them and through him send short notes to his staff. "I am so sorry that you have to suffer on our behalf," he wrote. "Don't be worried about your families. Our colleagues from the office in Peshawar are taking care of them."

The Afghan Shelter Now workers were held in strict confinement by the Taliban, intensively interrogated and beaten. In this way the Taliban tried to extract forced confessions, such as that they had been persuaded or otherwise bribed to become Christians. However, the employees remained steadfast and did not slander their employers.

One morning, from their cell, Georg and Peter noticed an old prison bus drive up and their 16 staff being loaded into it. Through their information channels they learned that they were taken to the notorious Pul-e-Charki prison, which held about 6,000 prisoners. And there they remained until November 13 when their guards fled before the approaching Northern Alliance troops and they were able to free themselves with the other inmates. Exactly what the Shelter Now colleagues had prayed almost daily came to pass, because they constantly feared that their staff would be hanged: "Lord God, if you deliver us out of the hands of the Taliban, then please free our Afghan staff before we are saved!"

REJECTION AND A WARM WELCOME

On his return to Kabul in the summer of 2002, Georg enjoyed the atmosphere and the new liberties on the streets of Kabul. He was able to visit friends without danger and go out with them to restaurants and amble through the streets, free from anxiety. On meeting up with old and trusted friends, however, he experienced an emotional roller coaster—some greeted him with joyful surprise, while on the faces of others he could read skepticism or rejection.

The Taubmann family went to the International Church on one of their first Sundays. They were looking forward to it, as colleagues from other aid agencies had returned and some of their friends attended regularly. Some of the congregation greeted them happily, though others held back and some even avoided them. When the person leading the service asked all to stand who were either first-time visitors or newly returned from overseas, he very deliberately passed over the Taubmanns and Silke. He simply didn't look in their direction, and they had to sit down again, embarrassed. The same happened in other places—but only with foreigners, never with local people. Their foreign acquaintances had obviously given credence to the media, which had given negative and false reports on the eight aid workers at the beginning of their imprisonment. Only a few were willing to change their opinion or to seek a clarifying conversation with Georg. It was not a pleasant experience for him.

In contrast to that, the reactions of the Afghans were quite different. Representatives of the Afghan Government heartily welcomed them and were really delighted that they had returned so quickly. Almost all of the 16 imprisoned staff, some of whom had also been tortured, returned to their organization and wanted to work for them again. Everywhere they came across Afghans who had had anything to do with them earlier, there were happy welcomes. Most of them were astounded that they had come back at all, despite the exertions, dangers and the looting of their offices, project facilities and houses. For many it was incomprehensible.

The governor of Khost, an educated man who had studied in Germany, arranged a reception in his home in Kabul. Georg had known him since 1992. In his area they had set up concrete factories to make girders and sold them at subsidized prices to the local population. More than 100,000 roof beams were provided to the residents of this province for a very reasonable price. Georg gave an address and the governor honored him in an official speech. Representatives of the Khost region also made the long journey to be present.

Afghan prisoners with whom he had been in prison and with whom he had developed friendships, visited him when they heard that Georg was back in Kabul. It was a special joy for Georg to meet Mashook again. Before their release, Mashook spent the last awful days with Georg in a cell in the dreaded secret service prison several meters underground, during the American bombardment.

Mashook was kidnapped with the eight Shelter Now aid workers and was to be taken to Kandahar. He was transported in the second vehicle. On the cold night in the container he gave Georg a warm blanket and a small pocket flashlight.

When fighting broke out on the way to Kandahar, he was able to escape his Taliban captor and walked the whole way back to Kabul, from where he reported the state of the hostages to the Afghan opposition forces, who had just entered the city of Kabul after the fall of the Taliban government on the same night. Now both of them were able to embrace and tell each other about their adventures.

Their friendship continues till today.

Georg Taubmann: Once I went to a UN gathering with different NGOs similar to ours, at which many Afghan colleagues were also represented. Unfortunately I arrived a little late. The event had already started. I opened the door quietly and tried to slip in without creating a disturbance. However, when the Afghans who were present saw me, they jumped up from their seats, rushed over to me, embraced me and gave me a loud welcome. The speaker couldn't continue. All the NGO representatives looked across at us amazed and wondered which important personage had entered. "Yes, don't you know, that's Mr. George from Shelter Now who was in prison and has just recently returned," it was explained to them.

Another time I was sitting in a government office and an Afghan colleague came in. He stopped short, broke into tears and hugged me tightly. "Mr. George, I cannot believe that you have come back. With all that you went through," he sobbed. It was the Afghans who had also suffered under the Taliban system who could identify most with what we had gone through, and were correspondingly thankful that we had returned.

During the course of 2002 the German Foreign Minister Joschka Fischer came with a delegation to Kabul. All the German NGOs were invited to a large gathering. They introduced themselves one after another. When it was Georg's turn, he said, "Georg Taubmann, Shelter Now International." A murmur went through the delegation. Joschka Fischer looked at him quite perplexed. "You? Are *you* Mr. Taubmann? Are you back again?"

His companion again asked, "Are you really the person who was imprisoned for three months by the Taliban?" The delegation could hardly take it in.

Mr. Fischer then remarked dryly, "Mr. Taubmann, you caused us a lot of headaches. Please look after yourself."

The former German Minister for Employment and Social Policy, Norbert Blüm, also arrived with a camera team from Stern-TV. The program was in aid of Children in Need. Georg had met Blüm in Peshawar and took him from the refugee camps there over the Khyber Pass to the Shelter Now projects in Afghanistan. Georg showed him the soup kitchens, which still provided for thousands of refugees, the cement works making concrete girders and the newly erected schools. It was an adventurous journey in the minibus through the Pashtun region, without any security personnel, and not entirely without risk. The camera team had plenty to do. Norbert Blüm was fascinated and very impressed, especially by the villages

Minister for Employment and Social Policy Norbert Blüm traveling from Peshawar to Kabul with Georg Taubmann

which had been completely destroyed by the Taliban and now were rebuilt with aid from Shelter Now—with houses, fruit trees, schools and the wells.

The trip ended in Kabul. There was a function at the German Embassy with the German Ambassador and representatives from the various UN organizations. Norbert Blüm was the speaker and praised the commitment of the Shelter Now team in most glowing terms. "I take my hat off to a man like Georg Taubmann," he said, "who was imprisoned by the Taliban and to our astonishment has returned to Afghanistan, and has again set up aid projects."

LOOKING BACK: IN THE SNARE OF THE RELIGIOUS POLICE

The accusation of the religious police against the four Germans, two Australians and two American development aid workers read: "Christian proselytization of Muslims." The various exhibits which they claimed to have seized were ridiculous: the DVD with the *Jesus* film, some Christian books and a crucifix, which belonged to none of them. Unfortunately, at the beginning of their imprisonment the press uncritically accepted the false accusations of the Taliban. Some presented Shelter Now as a Christian sect which helped others *only* in order to convert them to the Christian faith. Lastly, Shelter Now had only themselves to blame for their misfortune. Once these false statements spread, they stuck fast, as Georg himself sensed from foreign aid workers on his return to Kabul.

Only after the attack on the World Trade Center in New York on September 11, 2001, did it become clear to the world that the Shelter Now workers had been enticed into a trap set by the Taliban religious police. They were to be used as hostages in exchange for Al Qaeda terrorists and in negotiations with the US Government. Otherwise President Bush would not have demanded the unconditional extradition of Osama bin Laden and also specifically the release of the eight hostages.

In the following excerpt you can read how the arrest took place and what happened during the period when they were held hostage.

> As Afghans are normally very religious people, the Shelter Now people are often asked if they are Muslims or what they believe in. Because of that, conversations about faith arise quickly and spontaneously. As the Afghans do not see foreigners praying in public or practicing their religion, they often think that they do not believe in God (which they find totally incomprehensible), so they approach them about it. Whenever the fasting month of Ramadan comes around, the Shelter Now staff are asked what they think about fasting and praying, which gives rise to conversations about faith. Religion is a very important dimension in the life of Afghans, and when one has built a relationship with them, the conversation quickly revolves around faith, just as happens with us about sports, hobbies or politics.
>
> There are also many who are disappointed with their religion, after all that they have experienced with the Taliban. Then they want to know what Christians believe. Pastors in Pakistan have often told Georg that more and more Afghans are coming to their churches, wanting to become Christians, because they were disappointed with their religion. Once Georg was sitting in an international church in Peshawar, when an elderly Afghan couple sat down beside him. They spoke to him several times during the sermon, saying, "We want to become Christians.
> How do you do that?"

Excerpt from the book *Escape from Kabul*

Day 1: August 3, 2001

It is unlikely that the Shelter Now development workers will ever forget the first weekend of August 2001.

Since the foundation of Shelter Now in Peshawar in Northern Pakistan 18 years earlier, they had experienced hard times and life-threatening situations. But what they were about to experience that weekend had never occurred before.

The reason for their imprisonment and later prosecution had been the visit to an Afghan family. This family had badgered Katrin Jelinek, Heather Mercer and Dayna Curry many times to visit and to show them a documentary about the life of Jesus.

Katrin had gotten to know the children quite a while before—three girls and a boy aged roughly between four and twelve years. She had gone to their house regularly, in front of which she and Silke distributed food to street children. When the mother fell ill one day, the children had asked them to have a look at their sick mother. Katrin, a trained nurse, had brought some medication, and as is customary in Afghanistan they had had some tea and a chat.

Many Afghans are curious to know how Westerners live and whether they believe in God. In the West, faith is a private affair and it can be embarrassing to talk about it, but in the Muslim culture it is the most natural thing in the world to talk about one's faith. They want to know if the "*khoreji*," as the foreigner is called, believes anything at all and frequently they want to convince the infidel of their own Islamic faith. Muslims react in obvious astonishment when they realize that their guest is also a believer, though not in Allah, but in the God of the Bible.

And so it was with Katrin. When she responded to the woman's questions, she said that she believed in Jesus. Immedi-

> The Jesus documentary, which is available in many languages, had already been shown in some Islamic countries—excerpts were also later shown on Afghan TV. Much of what is portrayed in the film agrees with what a Muslim believes about the prophet (Isa) for whom he has great respect.

ately the women in the family wanted to know more about this prophet who is highly regarded in their religion. As they were not able to read, they had asked about a film.

On the aforementioned Friday afternoon in August, as Katrin Jelinek wanted to prepare for their planned volunteers' get-together that evening, she asked Heather Mercer and Dayna Curry to visit the Afghani family without her. And so it happened that it was only the two Americans who were sitting with the women and children, watching the documentary which they had requested on the laptop. The boy, who was very keen to learn English, was given a copy of a children's book in Dari and English by Dayna.

Dayna too had another appointment that afternoon and so left the family early and took a taxi to her destination. When the taxi had to stop briefly at a crossing, a man suddenly wrested open the passenger door and shouted threateningly at the driver, "Let me in!"

Dayna was shocked that the taxi driver simply allowed a strange man into the car, as she was sitting as a woman alone on the back seat.

"What do you think you're doing? Who are you?" the driver asked the stranger. "Shut your mouth!" he yelled at him and glared at Dayna with hate-filled eyes.

Then he took a walkie-talkie out and spoke into it, whereupon a second car full of Taliban fighters drove up beside them and someone with a weapon got in beside Dayna.

"Can you please take me to my people?" Dayna appealed to the driver. "I'm a woman. I am alone and I'm afraid."

But he just shrugged his shoulders in fear and his head sank. Suddenly a whole horde of Taliban surrounded the car.

"Where are the other women? Where is the equipment?" they bombarded Dayna with questions.

"I'm not speaking to you if you behave like this with me. I want to get to my organization!" she replied.

But they refused to listen to Dayna. For a good two hours she sat hunched in the vehicle, full of uncertainty. All sorts of thoughts raced through her head.

In this country, women on the streets were beaten and taken away for no reason. What did they intend to do with her? Dayna could do nothing except pray. After what seemed an eternity she saw another taxi arriving with Heather on the back seat, escorted by a car full of Taliban.

Heather had calmly finished watching the video with the family and at about 6 o'clock packed up her things. This time the farewell on the part of the family was not as effusive as usual.

As she walked across the plot of ground to the taxi, she wasn't accompanied by the women and the usual crowd of happy, noisy children. That surprised her a little, as did the presence of an unknown man sitting in the passenger seat of the taxi.

Funny, she thought. *Probably he was bored and asked a friend along.*

"Did I keep you waiting long?" she enquired.

She didn't receive an answer but caught sight of the driver's eyes wide with fright in the rearview mirror.

Scarcely had she sat down in the back seat, when the other door was opened and another man squeezed into the car.

Something's not right here! Alarmed, Heather was about to jump out of the taxi, but the fellow beside her grabbed her arm. In a flash the vehicle was surrounded by still more Taliban with Kalashnikovs and she was forced to go with them, for good or ill.

After a short drive they reached another taxi in which Heather saw her friend Dayna sitting. *Thank goodness, now at least I'm not alone*, she thought. Both were forced to get out and into another car. This was escorted by at least 30 armed Taliban, as they were taken to a women's prison.

Usually the Shelter Now colleagues trundled in to their regular Friday evening get-together at about 6 o'clock. For the first hour they mostly sat around chatting, drinking tea and eating snacks. At 7 o'clock the formal part of the evening began with announcements, work instructions and devotions.

"Hey, Georg, have you any idea what's happened to Heather and Dayna?" someone in the group asked. "They haven't come yet!"

"They're probably still visiting that family they told us about. They'll come later," he reassured them.

Still, it's strange, Georg thought to himself. *Oh well, visits like that always take longer than planned. Firstly, other relatives arrive, then the food isn't ready on time and before you know it, you're sitting there an hour or two longer than you intended.* With that, he dismissed his concerns.

During the devotions, however, Georg couldn't concentrate properly. An uncomfortable feeling nagged at him. It was the same with Margrit Stebner.

"Georg, we've got to do something," she urged him.

Katrin, who knew the house where the two girls were visiting, asked, "Shall I go quickly with Peter and Kurt and drop in on the family and check?"

"Yes please. We need to know what's happened!" replied Georg.

So that they wouldn't be conspicuous, the three of them didn't go in their own car, but took a taxi. When they arrived at the Afghan family's house, they found lots of confusion. The neighbors were standing around and talking nervously with one another.

"At least there are no Taliban around," Katrin reassured herself. They are always easy to recognize with their turbans and the inevitable Kalashnikovs.

After a while some women came up to them and spoke agitatedly to them in Dari. Kurt, who knew the language quite well, was able to gather from their anxious jabbering only the words: "Betrayal! Betrayal! They took the men as well!"

It became clear to the trio that something serious must have happened. Maybe Heather and Dayna were being interrogated or had possibly even been arrested. They quickly headed back to their colleagues' meeting.

When they burst into the group of their colleagues with this awful news, everyone was initially shocked and speechless. Georg quickly brought the meeting to a close and asked them to pray in small groups for Heather and Dayna.

After that he had Kurt and Jonathan drive him back to the Afghan family's house.

"Perhaps the women know more and can tell me who took them. And where they might have been taken to," he thought.

But the local women could not or would not give him any further information. So they went to the police station which was responsible for this part of the city. The officials on duty however were completely astounded and knew nothing.

At this point it was already 9 o'clock and curfew began at 11 pm. Georg wracked his brain. *Who on earth can help us?*

Haji Rashid! If there's anyone can help us, it's him, he suddenly thought with relief.

Haji Rashid was a top official in the Taliban, with whom Georg had developed a regular friendship in recent years. He would surely use his considerable influence on behalf of their two colleagues.

As the time for the curfew to begin was fast approaching, the three men raced along the streets of Kabul and in the darkness missed the Afghan's house. But they found his office right away. From there Georg took a guard with him just in case, and was shown the right road. So it was almost 10 pm when they reached his friend's house.

Georg Taubmann: In as relaxed a manner as is possible in such a situation, I stepped into my friend's house. With Afghans one must always spend lots of time in introductory niceties. Haji Rashid was delighted to see me.

He welcomed me with outstretched arms. "How are you and how is your family? Are you well?"

The typical Afghan greeting ceremony and the exchange of pleasantries began. We sat down and drank some tea. As I had just returned from quite a long stay in Germany, I told him about my family.

"And as a gift, I've brought you a blood pressure monitor, just like you asked me to," I cheerily informed him.

During my trip abroad he had had a traffic accident and now related it all in the greatest detail. In response I expressed my deep relief that nothing worse had happened to him.

Don't show any panic! Stay nice and calm! A quick glance at my wrist showed me that it was 10:30 pm.

Finally I plucked up courage and stated my concern. "Haji Rashid, something terrible has occurred in our NGO and I am very worried."

"My friend, tell me what has happened. Can I be of any assistance?"

"Yes. Two of my colleagues paid a visit to an Afghan family this afternoon and apparently have been arrested. I cannot find out where they are at the minute."

"Mr. George, that is dreadful. I understand your concern. I'll try right away to find out for you."

He went to the phone, dialed a number and conversed in a voice accustomed to authority. Meanwhile, I was watching his face. It became more and more pensive, concerned and, finally, appalled.

Haji Rashid replaced the receiver and came towards me with a horrified expression. "Mr. George, your two colleagues have indeed been arrested."

"But why?" I asked in despair.

"They say it's because they showed some films or other to Afghans. And it's the Religious Police of all people who have arrested them. I have no influence over them. That's an independent ministry which is under the control of Mullah Mohammed Omar. I was only able to warn them to treat the women decently."

"Haji Rashid, thank you very much for your friendly help. I am really very, very worried. Thank you for using your influence and helping us."

"But of course, my friend. I'm very glad to do that for you."

"May I come and see you again tomorrow? Maybe by then you'll have gotten some more information."

We arranged to meet again the following morning and said our polite farewells.

Once outside the three men quickly jumped into their car. It was now shortly before 11 pm and the curfew in Kabul was strictly observed. Anyone found by the Taliban on the streets after 11 pm could simply be arrested. In addition, Georg was not sure if the recent edict extending the curfew from 10 till 11 pm had gotten through to all the guards. With his head full of worries about the two women, and haunted by concerns about the time limit, he sped through the streets, always on the lookout for road checks. He turned into the entrance to his house with relief, just after 11 pm.

For Georg, it was a brief night, sleep couldn't have been further from his mind. His thoughts swirled continually around the same topics: *How are the two girls? Will other colleagues be interrogated? Are we threatened with further arrests? Should I evacuate all our colleagues? Oh God, what if our whole project is destroyed, like it was eleven years ago in Pakistan?*

Day 2: August 4, 2001

The next morning, a Saturday, there was one crisis meeting after another. At these, Georg asked his colleagues to prepare for a possible evacuation and to have their emergency luggage packed and ready.

"Please destroy anything which could be seen as offensive during a search by the Religious Police," he instructed his colleagues. "Remember that even advertisements in a German magazine can fall under that description!"

Over Radio Sharia, Mullah Omar was continually announcing new rules which could not possibly all be kept. For example, just recently Western women had been forbidden to drive. The actual law about wearing a burka did not apply to them, as they needed to be recognized as foreigners, but they were repeatedly abused and spat at by outraged Taliban for wearing only a chador (a large fabric headscarf). And naturally, individual colleagues had among their personal belongings Christian magazines, Bibles and music CDs in their own language, which was permissible. But even a copy of *Time* magazine or the journal *Stern* could be seen as offensive depending on the mood of the Religious Police.

Immediately after meeting with his colleagues, Georg went back again to his Afghan friend's office. He wasn't there, but his second-in-command was. The fact that a CD had indeed turned up in the aforementioned Afghan house and that the Religious Police were behind the arrest, gave him also great cause for concern. He was torn between his personal friendship with Georg and anxiety that he himself would be harassed by the Religious Police. He couldn't help them any further. So Georg requested him to give to Heather and Dayna a bag with some personal items.

Back in the office Georg contacted friends throughout the world, asking them to pray about the critical situation. They phoned Heather and Dayna's relatives and churches. The organization's offices in Pakistan and Germany were also informed.

An oppressive atmosphere hung over the whole day and into the evening. Yet the hustle and bustle and the increased workload were a welcome distraction from the ever-present anxiety about the future.

Day 3: August 5, 2001

Early on Sunday morning at 6 o'clock the front doorbell on Georg Taubmann's house sounded loudly. His wife Marianne went down and peered cautiously through the peephole.

"Can we speak to Mr. George?" asked one of the Afghans who was standing at the door. "It's urgent!"

"Georg, come quickly! There's a jeep full of men outside!"

Fearing the worst, Georg hurried outside and opened the gate. But it was Afghan friends who were standing outside. They seemed anxious and in a great hurry.

"Mr. George, we have information that your offices will be searched today. And it's going to get even worse."

Georg sensed that this news was reliable and thanked them. Hastily they drove away.

In spite of all the evil that is happening to us, there are still some good people among the Taliban, he thought to himself.

At 8 o'clock the colleagues met in Diana and Margrit's house.

"I have reliable information that our main office will be searched today," he shared with them. "It may well be that they'll also search other houses. Be ready for evacuation."

At this point no one suspected further arrests.

"Please see to the most pressing concerns and we'll meet again here in the house at 2 o'clock for our next team meeting," he told them as they left. But this meeting would never take place. Events came tumbling over them in quick succession over the next few hours. First, Diana Thomas and Margrit Stebner were arrested by the Religious Police in front of the administration office just as they were about to withdraw their private funds and some documents from the safe. Diana managed to send a warning by radio which other colleagues heard many times.

Upon hearing this, Peter Bunch left immediately with the leader of the Afghan Project to check what was going on. The two of them were promptly arrested. They were allowed to drive themselves to prison, as the Taliban had no vehicles.

Shortly before the 2 o'clock rendezvous, Katrin Jelinek checked in on the children's homes to make sure everyone was well. She wanted to give the Afghan employees some instructions and leave them some money in case she had to leave Kabul. But she was intercepted by the Taliban there and was forced to lead them to her residence. Here her roommate, Silke Dürrkopf, who was ill, was hauled out of bed by armed Taliban.

After his visit to the Afghan Foreign Ministry, it had occurred to Georg that he should call on Katrin and Silke on the way back, to ensure that they were okay. He shouldn't have done so. A group of Taliban were still keeping guard over the building. They dragged him into their vehicle and hauled him off for questioning.

Margrit Stebner: There really was something in the air. To know that two of your colleagues have been arrested is a bitter pill to swallow. You begin to ask yourself what it would be like if it happened to you.

In late afternoon Diana and I intended to quickly fetch a few personal papers, and more especially our own private funds, from the office safe. We had gone there by taxi. When we arrived however, the gate was locked and a group of Taliban were standing there.

Not suspecting anything, we asked them, "Can we go into the office and fetch a few things?"

"Wait here. Someone's just getting the key for the entrance," the leader responded. So we sent the taxi away and waited. In Afghanistan, one must always have patience. After a good half-hour had elapsed, we got fed up. As the taxi had gone, we went back down the little street. But we didn't get far. Some men ran after us; we tried to ignore them. When one of them with a whip barred our way, then we knew: we're now caught as well!

"You're not allowed to leave," said the Talib with the whip. "Stay here at the gate. You're going to be interrogated. We're waiting for the vehicle."

There was no longer any doubt; the two of us were also under arrest. As we were tired standing, we squatted down on the ground at the gate. More than an hour went by without anything at all happening.

While we were waiting, panic was spreading through my limbs and all sorts of horrendous pictures were going through my head—of women being beaten and abused. Of dark dungeons. We prayed quietly. That calmed me and after a few minutes the awful pictures disappeared from my thoughts.

At one point, Diana, as inconspicuously as possible, was brave enough to place her walkie-talkie to her mouth and say, "Hi, everybody. We are in front of our administration office and the Taliban won't let us go…."

But straight away, one of the guards spied the radio and grabbed it from her. The group of Taliban sat about 20 meters from us, observing us contemptuously.

They were mostly young men with black or white turbans on their heads and dark, sunburned faces. Some were dressed in black, others in white salwar kameezes (the typical traditional dress consisting of wide trousers and a long shirt). Then one of the young fellows stood up, fooling around with his Kalashnikov and came towards us.

Watch out, Margrit, he's about to take aim and shoot the both of you, an inner voice told me, *but he'll miss.*

"Thank you, Lord," I whispered and prodded Diana. "Look out, that fellow's about to shoot."

And indeed, he lifted his gun, aimed at us—and the bullets whizzed just past our heads.

Diana and I ignored him. "We're not going to give the Talib the satisfaction of intimidating us," both of us thought. We were furious with these blokes and at the same time thankful that we had been prepared for this tricky situation. Otherwise we wouldn't have been able to react in such a levelheaded way.

Every volunteer carried a -talkie with a range of up to five kilometers. Peter heard Diana's radio message, grabbed Gul Khan, their Afghan Project Manager, and drove to the office. As they were approaching the building, they noticed that something was wrong, from the presence of a group of Taliban.

"Keep going!" Gul Khan shouted to Peter.

Peter pressed the accelerator, for the Taliban were already running towards them.

They could easily have escaped, but the thought went through his head, *But what about the girls? I cannot simply abandon them. They're in real difficulty. I've got to help them!*

So he turned around and drove right up to the Taliban. At once the mob surrounded him and stuck their Kalashnikovs through the side windows. They seized his radio and demanded the car keys. Peter resisted as long as he could, but, confronted by the weapons, he reluctantly handed over the keys.

Then he tried bargaining with them. "Let the women go! What's all this about? They're only office workers!"

But nothing doing! They pushed Margrit and Diana and as many guards as possible into their vehicle, and the Shelter Now volunteers were permitted to drive in their own vehicle to the prison for their cross-examination.

Silke Dürrkopf: On the weekend in question, I was ill with stomach problems and spent most of the time in bed. I had just returned to Afghanistan a few days earlier after a 10-week stay in Germany.

As I'd found the many team meetings that weekend quite exhausting, I took advantage of the midday break to rest. I was awakened by unusual voices and noises, in the midst of which I could hear Katrin's voice.

Just a minute, something's not quite right, I thought. *You'd better get dressed properly.*

I had just pulled on my salwar kameez when the door burst open and at least ten armed men stormed in.

Again I thought, *This is outrageous! I haven't even got my head covered with my chador.* I was incredibly ashamed and furious. By Western standards, of course, I was decently dressed, but not according to Pashtun standards.

Incensed, I let the intruders have it—in three languages at once—chased them out of my room and banged the door in their faces. At that moment, I wasn't in the least concerned about the Kalashnikovs. I simply wanted the chance to dress properly.

Outside the door, Katrin was reassuring the agitated men and explaining my outraged reaction. And they actually did allow me a few minutes to throw on my chador before stepping out of the room.

The leader asked me my name and whether I had anything to do with Shelter Now. From that I ascertained that they didn't know me at all and that I must have crossed their path purely by accident.

"You two come with us! We have a few questions. It'll only take one or two hours. Then you can leave," they lied to us.

And so we followed them down the stairs. Just then it suddenly occurred to me, *You should take your money with you!*

I turned on my heel, hurried into the room and quickly stuffed my little cloth purse which held the dollar bills into my pocket. Of course the leader sent a Talib after me, but fortunately he didn't catch on to what was in the little bag.

As it's difficult to transfer money in Afghanistan, I had brought a load of cash with me from Germany, which then sustained my fellow prisoners and me during our long imprisonment. Fortunately the little cloth purse was of no interest to anyone in future inspections.

Okay then, I thought to myself, *I've only been back in Kabul for a few days. This must be a huge misunderstanding.*

I was definitely hoping that nothing would happen to me, for the stamp in my passport was, after all, unmistakable proof of a recent short stay.

Georg Taubmann: I was unaware of the arrests on the Sunday morning. When I was driving past Katrin and Silke's house on the way to our 2 o'clock meeting, I saw a group of Taliban hanging about in front of their house.

That's strange, I thought. *What's going on here?*

Astonished, I got out of the car. Immediately the group stormed up to me and surrounded me.

"Are you Mr. George?"

"I am Mr. Taubmann," I replied, confusing them somewhat and gaining a little time to think.

"What's the matter?"

They seized me roughly and pulled me into the girls' house. The whole place was teeming with Taliban. I was shattered and knew right away that Katrin and Silke had probably been arrested.

After a short discussion, of which I understood nothing, they snatched my car keys, dragged me to my car and pushed me onto the passenger seat. A guard tried to squeeze in beside me, which made it impossible to close the door.

They therefore hauled me violently out of the car again, tore at my clothing and threw me roughly onto the back seat. Passers-by watched this brutal scene, horrified and intimidated. They then raced through the streets in my vehicle, with me behind them wedged in between my guards. They pulled me forcibly into an office of the Religious Police, dragging me along violently and treating me like a common criminal.

It is dreadful to suddenly be a prisoner. No concern, no respect was shown me. Whenever I had gone previously to any state institution or authority, I had always been respected as a foreigner and as Director of a reputable aid project. But these people looked at me contemptuously.

At some point I sat in a rather large office with several desks. About 15 Afghans were also there, among them some wild looking young men. The latter gave me a questionnaire to fill out: name, age, father's name, grandfather's name, address, how long in Afghanistan, what business, etc. One of the first questions they asked me was, "How many teachers have you employed in your madrassa? What are their names?"

"What? How? Madrassa?" I couldn't understand what they were looking for.

"We don't have a religious school! We don't have any teachers either! We have only a project for giving boys some work and something to eat," I answered.

"No, no! That's not correct. You must tell us how many teachers you have employed and what their names are!"

They simply wouldn't believe me.

Of course there were lots more questions: "How many projects do you have?

Where are they located? How many colleagues are working with you? What are they called? Where do they live? Where are the other Americans?"

I was on my guard and at first named only those who I knew had already been arrested. I wanted to protect the others. Things were quite frantic in this first interrogation.

Then suddenly the door opened and Peter Bunch was brought in. Happy to see me, he was about to rush up to me but was held back.

"You are not permitted to speak to each other!" they ordered roughly. So he had to go and squat down at the other end of the room and fill out the same questionnaire as I had.

Then I noticed our Afghan workers being led in. I was able to count eight of them: our faithful project manager, engineers, drivers, a cook and some watchmen. They looked very crushed and anxious. My heart was heavy, because they could certainly expect brutal questioning. It was unbearable to think about. They were led past us and into another room.

In retrospect, more pieces of the puzzle fit together to reveal a pre-planned trap by the Religious Police: the Afghan ladies were very insistent in their request to see the *Jesus* film. When leaving the house, the development aid worker was not, as is generally the case, accompanied to the street by the children and the women. Clearly they had known about the planned arrest. The fact that the Afghan family were not arrested at the same time as their visitors is an unambiguous indication that they were used by the Religious Police and put under pressure to invite the aid workers and to persuade them to show the film.

When they were arrested, the Taliban continually asked for further names of Americans. They obviously wanted to get as many Americans as possible under their control as hostages.

Why did they destroy the majority of their aid projects one day after the arrest of the Shelter Now teams? Why did they loot their houses a short time later and not await the outcome of the court proceedings? Surely it was because the elimination of the aid organization had been already decided and it was all a show trial on the part of the Taliban.

IF ONLY A CAR COULD SPEAK

During the majority of his 16 years in Pakistan and then in Afghanistan, Georg mostly drove his beloved silver Pajero Jeep. He had taken it over from his predecessor in Pakistan. If only the jeep could speak, it would have some very dramatic tales to tell…

Georg Taubmann: I have already reported how, on our arrest on August 5, 2001, the Taliban robbed us of all our possessions and destroyed our offices, our private homes, the cement works and also our fleet of vehicles, including my service vehicle, the silver-colored Pajero Jeep.

After our return to Kabul in the spring of 2002, we were just setting up our offices and private homes, when two of our Afghan colleagues came to me very excited and shouted, "Mr. George, Mr. George, we have seen your silver Pajero."

"How? What? That can't be true," I replied.

"Yes, yes! Definitely! We'll keep our eyes peeled and see that you get it back."

They did indeed recognize the jeep in road traffic and followed it. It emerged that an adviser to the Afghan President Karsai was the new owner. We were able to prove that the vehicle belonged to Shelter Now and got it back without any difficulty. It had even undergone a thorough inspection in the meantime and had two new tires. We became friendly with the adviser; we visited one another and he told us how he had come by the car. At the liberation of Kabul by the Northern Alliance, some Taliban had presumably fled in the jeep to Khost District and left it standing there.

The ownerless vehicle was brought

Georg Taubmann in his beloved Pajero Jeep

back to Kabul and eventually came into the keeping of this adviser.

I drove this jalopy around for years in Kabul. But the steering wheel was on the right hand side, as we had acquired it and driven it in Pakistan. Later such cars were no longer permitted in Afghanistan, so we handed over the faithful jalopy to our colleagues there.

The vehicle had a long history. In 1990 it already belonged to Shelter Now and our leader at that time drove it. He and his son miraculously escaped an attempted murder in this vehicle. He was driving just outside Peshawar when he was shot at by would-be assassins with two Kalashnikovs. He received a flesh-wound, and his son was unharmed, but the bodywork was peppered with shots, the windshield destroyed, and the bullets stuck in the upholstery and the spare tire. Our leader was in shock. He went back to America with his wife and family, and the work in Pakistan was halted for a short time. I took over the leadership and got the wrecked Pajero as my service vehicle. With great care we filled in the bullet holes, sandpapered them carefully and had the jeep newly sprayed. Even though the vehicle looked perfect again from the outside, I was always reminded when I got into it of the awful thing that had happened in it.

In the years when we led the new aid projects in Afghanistan from our base in Pakistan, this all-purpose vehicle frequently traveled the stretch from Peshawar to Kabul and back. Although it was only 280 kilometers, the roads were extremely poor and full of deep potholes which had to be circumvented. Many bridges had been destroyed, so we had to drive through the rivers. Nearly the whole time one could only drive in first or second gear. So it was extremely tiring for us. I had to admire the jeep, how it constantly brought us to our goal, in spite of a few breakdowns.

This jeep remained my trusty companion when we moved to Kabul in 2000. During the Taliban period I drove it in Kabul. On the day of my arrest too! I wanted to see how our two women colleagues were doing, drove to their place and got out.

Immediately a group of Taliban, who were squatting in front of the house opposite, ran up to me. They seized me, tore open the back door and forcibly shoved me in. On each side of me there was a Talib. One of the Taliban sat behind the steering wheel and drove me to prison in my own jeep.

To me it's a source of amused wonder that I was able to sit behind the wheel of my faithful, beloved Pajero again after my return to Kabul, and that it accompanied me for many more years.

A NEW HOME IN KABUL

Georg Taubmann: When we went to Kabul again in June 2002, we lived temporarily in a house abandoned by a female colleague, and had two rooms there. The search for a new house proved to be difficult, as the rents had risen horrendously after the liberation from the Taliban. We would have loved to have returned to our old house, but we learned that it was already rented out to someone else. We thought about our old home a lot. What might it look like now? The house had been like an oasis for us during the Taliban period. We enjoyed living there and had furnished it very nicely. We were longing to see it again. We knew that it would be difficult emotionally, but we wanted to see what was left of it. In addition some of our things were still hidden there.

It was June and our contract ran until August, because before our arrest we had paid a year in advance. We set out as a family. We knocked hesitantly at the door. An American lady opened the door and looked at us curiously and suspiciously. "Hello, we are the Taubmanns. We lived in this house before you. Actually it's still our house as we paid the rent up till August."

The woman was quite shocked and explained to us that she knew nothing about it. Her American organization had rented it. She knew the story of the eight aid workers who had been imprisoned by the Taliban, and was even more surprised to learn that I was the leader of the group. She looked rather confused, as she realized that we were actually the legal tenants. Curious, I asked her what the rent was. "My organization pays 4000 dollars a month," she replied. My mouth fell open. Before we were taken hostage, we paid exactly 200 dollars per month. It became painfully obvious to me that we couldn't have moved in here anyway, at these prices.

After a little hesitation, I asked her, "May we come in and have a look around?" There was nothing left of our furnishings. Everything had been looted and destroyed by the Taliban. The landlord had completely refurbished the house. With heavy hearts and disappointment we looked around. Still, it had once been our lovingly furnished home, equipped with personal memorabilia and gifts from dear friends.

The two boys asked if they might be allowed to climb up to the roof-space. The new occupants didn't know that there was a hatch there. Like a flash both of them disappeared up into the attic. They returned triumphantly with a bundle of CDs and videos. On their precipitous departure from Kabul they had quickly hidden them there, so that they didn't fall into the hands of the Taliban. Daniel and Benjamin were super-happy and the tenants completely perplexed but also concerned about all that we had lost. Sadly and with heavy hearts we said goodbye and left. We had indeed lost everything that we possessed, most of all, our home. A small consolation was the treasure which the two boys had found under the roof.

AN UNEXPECTED TEST

Georg Taubmann: We had just been back in Kabul for a few weeks, when the doorbell of our new house rang one morning.

I opened the door. There stood a young man with a beard, not quite as long as the Taliban's beards. He looked at me earnestly and greeted me. I was quite surprised. "Who are you, and what do you want?" I asked.

"Do you not know me?" replied my visitor. "No, how should I know you?"

He gave me a hint: "I was one of the guards in the prison."

With that, I recognized him and the scenes in the prison played out before my eyes. Frightened, and absolutely shocked that a simple Talib knew where I lived, I asked with narrowed eyes, "What do you want?"

"Can you not give me a job?"

I found that so bare-faced that I just stared back at him without a word. I had expected that he would maybe apologize for what had happened in the prison, or perhaps say, "Great, that you're still alive. Welcome back to Afghanistan." No, he just blatantly wanted a job from me. I was really annoyed. I gave a sharp response, "No, we don't have any jobs." I turned away and shut the door in annoyance. That was very rude in Afghan culture. I was all churned up and told Marianne, "Can you imagine? A Taliban guy, who had previously kept guard over me in prison, was standing at the door, didn't even say sorry and wants a job from me. Outrageous!"

I realized that I found it hard to forgive certain people. I remembered my words at our first press conference in Islamabad, when I said that we would forgive those who had done us so much harm. Now I wasn't behaving like that. Full of regret, I prayed that God would give me the strength to forgive people like this also. The next day the doorbell rang again, and the guy was standing at the door once more. This time I was able to meet him in a more composed way. I explained to him in a polite Afghan manner that I had no work for him, as our organization had not yet been rebuilt and said a respectful goodbye. Test passed!

The underground Taliban in Kabul knew that Georg Taubmann was back. The former Talib whom Georg knew from the prison as a guard and who called on him asking for work, was a clear indication of that. A friendly Afghan, who had contact with the Taliban, confirmed to Georg that the Taliban knew of his return and were watching him.

In the Khost region and in Kandahar, Shelter Now was rebuilding our precast concrete factories. This town was quickly infiltrated again by the Taliban. In Kandahar they even came to the concrete factories and bought concrete girders. They knew that Shelter Now was back and they could have attacked the foreign staff at any time. One time there was a critical situation when a Talib threatened a Shelter Now worker. They appealed to his boss, who had already obtained roof girders from them, and the boss personally put him firmly in his place.

THE FIRST PROJECT IN SHAMALIE

It wasn't easy to get the Shelter Now projects going again, working out from Kabul. The old offices had been ransacked. New ones had to be found which were also affordable. Rents had skyrocketed, because so many other organizations, embassies and UN agencies needed premises. The renovation and refurbishment of office space cost time and took a lot of effort. To get the ruined projects up and going again required laborious, detailed work.

The first project that Shelter Now set up again was in Shamalie, to the

North of Kabul. In 1998 this district was conquered by the Taliban, the villages destroyed and the inhabitants driven out. Although the area was retaken, the Taliban came again in 2000 and committed a dreadful massacre. Many men were killed, their women kidnapped. The fruit trees were hacked down, the irrigation plants and wells ruined. Their means of livelihood were simply destroyed. The survivors fled to Pakistan, where they were crammed into massive tented villages in the desert by the government, far from any town. Shelter Now undertook the task of providing them promptly with drinking water and a regular supply of food.[5]

First provision of drinking water for newly arrived refugees, who have to live in tents

A further step was to set up medical care and schools. With the high temperatures and desert dust storms, tents eventually present undignified living conditions, so Shelter Now, together with the refugees, specialized in the construction of mud houses which offer good protection from the heat in summer and from the cold in winter. This resulted in work opportunities for the refugees; they received the building materials and tools and built the houses themselves. The construction of a mud house cost exactly the same as a tent. In this way thousands of houses were erected in the camps. In addition, many of these refugees were regularly supplied with food and water for years by Shelter Now.

In addition to soup kitchens, bakeries are constructed in which the refugees can bake their own bread

The refugees live in tents as well as in mud houses built by Shelter Now

Due to a shortage of wood, concrete girders for roof construction are produced in cement factories set up by Shelter Now

A man building his mud house; each of the 20-meters-square houses consists of one room with an attached toilet

In recent years Shelter Now provided material for thousands of mud houses

> The Afghan refugees who moved to Pakistan were collected in desert-like conditions outside the cities and were accommodated initially in tents. In these places the temperature soars to 50 degrees C. during the summer months. As the women may not leave the tents for cultural reasons, they and the children suffer the most. There were always many deaths.
>
> On one occasion the Pakistani Commissioner for Refugees rang Georg, quite distraught. He had looked into a tent on one of his official visits and caught sight of a woman who was almost unconscious with a dead child in her arms. "Please, Mr. George," he pleaded, "please build more of these mud houses. We cannot get enough of them."

When the Taliban regime fell in Afghanistan in 2001, and the Taliban were driven out of many areas, the tribal leaders of the refugees from Shamalie who were housed in refugee camps outside Peshawar, turned to Georg in Kabul and requested him to help them rebuild their villages, so that they could finally leave the wretched refugee camps. The whole area was completely destroyed and razed to the ground, the most serious aspect being that without any well water there was no possibility of reconstruction.

Georg agreed; and so the reconstruction of the villages around Shamalie became the first project after setting up the office in Kabul. The refugees returned. First of all, a factory for concrete girders and roof tiles was erected where the villagers could get work right away and start rebuilding their own houses.[6] Later came the production of concrete pillars for vineyards. Hundreds of houses and three schools were built. Each family received girders, roof tiles, as well as window and doorframes from Shelter Now, so that they could build their own houses. It

> On returning to Shamalie from the refugee camp in Pakistan, a whole series of families loaded the doors of their mud houses onto the trucks. SNI and the names of the donor agencies were written large on the doors. Now these inscriptions could be seen on many houses in Shamalie.

was this project that had so impressed Norbert Blüm on his trip.

The wells and water installations were speedily restored. As all the animals had been slaughtered, Shelter Now began a project whereby cows were distributed to the families. These were later paid for, so that other families also had the opportunity to apply for cows.[7] As the families had no foodstuffs after their return, they were regularly provided with food by Shelter Now until they brought in their first harvest.

Georg Taubmann: I found it very moving to see the old doors with the Shelter Now logo on the new houses. It reminded me of a part of our history. Now we were helping the very same people whom we had helped years before with initial care, to build a proper new home. When I traveled through Afghanistan it often happened that tribal elders would greet me with deep respect, saying, "We know each other from the refugee camps in Pakistan. Our children drank the milk that you distributed. You helped us to survive." Many of those who returned after 2002 had had to live in refugee camps for up to 20 years—and during that time were provided for by Shelter Now.

SHELTER NOW WOMEN RETURN TO KABUL

All three German aid workers announced at their release that they intended to return to Kabul. Silke Dürrkopf was the first to achieve this by accompanying the Taubmann family in 2002, first to Peshawar and then on to Kabul. She remained until 2004, taught Benjamin, and worked in the newly furnished office in Kabul.

Margrit Stebner stayed for some months in Germany and gave many talks about their experiences in prison. In October 2002 she too flew to Kabul and remained with Shelter Now for five years. She worked mainly in administration, was responsible for looking after guests and was Georg's personal secretary. In 2007 she realized a long held dream by beginning to serve in a Middle Eastern country. The reason she gave: "I just sensed that my time with Shelter Now was at an end and a new step in my vocation was calling."

Margrit Stebner: For me it was clear from the beginning that I would go back. Otherwise it would have been like an incomplete chapter in the story of my life. I had a task to do there and wanted to finish it. I definitely wanted to return and have never regretted it—even though it was a challenging time, especially at the beginning.

I couldn't get back into my old apartment. It had been occupied and ransacked by the Taliban. Like the others, I had to make a completely new start: new accommodation, new furniture, new household equipment. At first I rented a room in a friend's house. Later I was able to move into a little house on the same plot as the Taubmanns, directly beside them. I could easily entertain guests there. It was very pleasant to be living nearby.

Right after my arrival it struck me that the atmosphere in the city was quite changed. There was life on the streets, as is normal in the Orient. The bazaars were bursting with goods and people. There was laughter and loud music. That hadn't been possible under the Taliban; it was like a ghost town then. When I think back, 60% of Kabul was destroyed. There was no infrastructure, ruined streets everywhere, no telephone, no mail. Unbelievable how everything had changed.

The security situation too was different in my first two years back in Kabul. Of course, one must always have one's antenna up for various situations. I lived constantly in a state of alertness, but fortunately I'm not an over-anxious person. You can't be if you're going to live there.

In 2004-2005 however, one could sense increasing resistance from the Taliban. Also, a certain discontent and disappointment among the Afghans. Many had imagined that the reconstruction would have been easier. For most people circumstances did not improve as quickly as hoped, which fanned the flames of discontent among the population. The Taliban had newly re-formed and begun to stir up resistance against both Afghan and foreign troops. Foreigners and aid organizations also became the enemy and were targeted. Suicide attacks were new and devastating, which had not been the case earlier.

I actually did well emotionally after my return to Kabul. The mood of optimism was infectious and we had so many more opportunities. I visited the old places with the others: the prisons, the Supreme Court, Saidabad, where we spent a night in the container. The last three days especially before our release were really stark, somehow surreal.

The journey towards Kandahar, the unexpected liberation in Ghazni and the crazy helicopter story. It had all happened so quickly that I carried a "wild" picture of the events in my head. It felt until then as if I had emerged from an action film. Seeing the places and the people again, remembering and talking about it, helped me to be more grounded about our story. Some time during this period I had decided in my mind, that the three-and-a-half months of being a hostage should not define me. I also didn't want to construct an identity as a Taliban hostage. That's why it was important for me to go back, crazy as it may sound. I was no longer beholden to others, as I was in prison, but could be active, change something – that was a victory for me.

Some years later, however, when I'd been back in Germany for a long time, I did have so-called body flashbacks for a short period. Whenever I lay down to sleep, the bombs came. Real waves of detonation went through my body and the scenes during the bombings of Kabul went through my mind. I saw myself lying in the dark corridor of the prison, the walls were shaking, and as the prison took a direct hit, there was no chance of escape. However, an EMDR (Eye Movement Desensitization and Reprocessing) treatment helped me to overcome these traumatic experiences.

There was plenty for Margrit to do in the office. They were a small team, maybe nine or ten people, and had large projects to manage. On the basis of worldwide assistance for the reconstruction of Afghanistan, huge sums of money were placed at their disposal; these had to be administered and invested well. "One project excited me especially. The project 'Villages of Hope' which Len Stitt, the team leader had devised and was carrying out in the Shamalie plain," Margrit remembers. The project involved lots of work in its preparation and implementation. On top of that, Margrit was responsible for personnel questions and applications, as well as the care of guests and sponsors and, as Georg's personal assistant, kept an overview of his correspondence, appointments and activities.

Margrit Stebner: It was a very busy time. Everyone was in an optimistic mood. There was neither boredom nor too much leisure time. We had lots of guests and the intercultural staff increased steadily. A team consisting of 13 different nationalities brings with it a special dynamic and a high conflict potential. That wasn't always easy for Georg to handle. The team situation and the high workload often brought many to their limits. And as secretary I was caught between two stools and bore the brunt of it. Or I took on so many extra tasks that really didn't belong to my sphere of responsibility.

A special highlight for me was the annual commemoration get-together in November with the Afghan colleagues who had been imprisoned at the same time as we had. We celebrated with a lovely meal, and whoever wished had the opportunity to share. We wanted to express our appreciation of our Afghan colleagues and hear about their experiences.

In the two years before Georg founded the international office in Sulzbach-Rosenberg, Germany, he oscillated a lot between Kabul and Germany, and I followed him. So I had a small apartment in a village neighboring Sulzbach-Rosenberg, and in Kabul I had a room in a shared house with three women. When the international office was set up, it was time for me to go to Israel.

Katrin Jelinek did not return to Kabul until 2007, now with the surname Lohser, as she had married Thomas in October 2002. It was always the desire of her heart to continue her projects in Afghanistan. At the beginning of 2003 she flew to Kabul with Thomas to spend a week there. She wanted to show Thomas her old surroundings and Thomas wanted to have a clearer picture as to whether they could work together there.

Katrin Lohser: The week was full of impressions and experiences. When we arrived in Kabul, I was astonished at the changes. Outwardly there still wasn't much to see, but the crippling fear of the Taliban was broken and that could be felt in the city and among the citizens. In conversations we could pick up hope for a better future than there had been before.

Although only a year had passed since our release, there was already a Shelter Now team again in Kabul. Georg, Margrit and Silke had been living for almost a year in the country and other overseas colleagues had joined them. We were very warmly received by them, and Thomas had the chance to get to know them better. Over the next few days he got a good insight into life in Kabul.

Together with Georg, Margrit and Silke, we visited "our" prisons, telling Thomas the stories about them. In addition, he learned about the various projects of Shelter Now. At the end, Thomas had a good experience which made quite an impact on him. "On the final day we went to Kabul University. As an engineer, I wanted to find out about the Uni as well as the possibility of working there at some point. Without anything having been planned, we were passed through various hoops by a secretary, right up to the University President, and were able to converse with him for almost half an hour. He received us with open arms. The Afghans seem to hold us Germans in high esteem—and, of course, the aid which comes from Germany. I asked the President whether I would be able to teach at the University, if I were to come back to Kabul in one or two years' time. He believed he could support that. I just thought, *Really, doors couldn't open any wider!*"

After their return, Thomas continues to work at his profession as an engineer. Katrin takes some further courses and has two children. Then at last they are ready to go. In spring 2007, they decamp from Germany and fly to Kabul. The children are two and three years old. They quickly settle in as a family. Thomas is asked if he would like to assume leadership of the team in Kabul after 2008.

They agree hesitantly, as they still see themselves as inexperienced newcomers. But then Thomas becomes seriously ill. He has to return to Germany very suddenly for treatment. Katrin follows with the children in February 2008. A lengthy period of ill health follows, with the result that they are no longer in a position to pursue their service in Kabul. After his recovery they devote themselves to activities in Germany.

A Change in Family Life

2001 was a challenging year for the Taubmann family, full of death threats and much anxiety. In 2002 that was to be repeated. This time it didn't hit Georg but one of his sons, 16-year-old Daniel. On precisely the first anniversary of Georg's imprisonment, August 5, 2002, the boarding school in Pakistan which Daniel had been attending for only a week, was attacked by Taliban terrorists with the aim of murdering all the students. By a miracle, students and teachers were spared— unfortunately some watchmen and employees lost their lives.

After this tragic event a period of living separately began for the Taubmann family. Up until then they had always been able to live together. In Peshawar, the children went to a local school or had private instruction through distance learning. In Kabul, Silke continued her individual instruction. When some of Daniel's friends in Kabul decided in the summer of 2002 to go to a Christian International School in the mountains, in Murree, Pakistan, he joined them.

Benjamin was to continue his individual learning with Silke. That was not easy for Benni, without his brother

The attack on the school horrified the overseas employees of the NGOs. Many organizations closed down their work and left the country. The school relocated to Chiang Mai in Thailand. Daniel went there till his final school year in 2004.

Happily for Benjamin, he was able to move to Chiang Mai some time later, and live with his brother in a residence for boarding school students. He, though, went to another school, the German Christian Overseas School, as the German system suited him better. Marianne too lived for six months in Chiang Mai and was able to take on the job of a house mother during this period.

After finishing school, the three moved to Germany. And so began a period of living separately and of frequent change, back and forth between Germany and Kabul.

ATTACK ON THE BOARDING SCHOOL IN PAKISTAN

Georg Taubmann: Marianne, Benni and I accompanied Daniel to his new school. The school year began in August and we set out at the end of July. This is the hottest time of year. The school was situated in the mountains in the North of Pakistan, about an hour's journey by car from Islamabad, with a pleasant climate, so we rented a holiday home nearby and intended to drive Daniel to and from the school each day during our vacation.

On August 5th, Daniel had been going to the school for a week. I said to Marianne, "Today is the first anniversary of my capture. I'd like to withdraw and pray and think through a few things. Today especially, so many memories have been set off. Please, can you see that I'm not disturbed?"

There I am, sitting in my room and trying to sort out my thoughts and emotions. About an hour later Marianne comes rushing into the room, distraught. "Georg, Georg, there's just been a call from the school! They've been attacked by terrorists! I don't know any more."

Marianne has scarcely finished when I run to our car and race down the mountain to the school. It takes about 15 minutes. I run up to the door at the entrance and see the first blood-soaked corpse lying there. Carefully, I go through the entrance; the watchman's hut is full of blood. The watchman must have been hit. Indescribable panic rises within me. *What about the children? How is Dani? Where can he be?*

I go across to the church which stands on the left at the beginning of the building complex; it serves also as a multipurpose hall and is used for lessons and

> When the Taliban regime fell in Afghanistan in December 2001, thousands of Pakistani Taliban moved back to Pakistan. Almost immediately, attacks on Christian institutions began. In March there was an attack on the International Christian Church in Islamabad. A suicide bomber blew himself up inside the church building. Then many mission hospitals and individual Christians were attacked. The school administration and Georg also were privately very concerned that the school could be hit, as there were many foreign children— approximately 150. On the one hand, they told each other that it was inconceivable that the terrorists would attack children, but on the other, everyone knew how brutal the Taliban could be. The school had already taken further precautionary measures: they had strengthened the security personnel, the entrance area was more strictly controlled, they had increased the height of the walls and installed a watchtower.

sport such as basketball. When I enter through the door, I see a group of terrified children and also teachers. Shock and fear are written across their faces. I discover Daniel, he runs to me, clings to me and I try to comfort him.

More details emerged later. In total, there were six terrorists who stormed the school. Five employees and a man who happened to be passing the entrance were killed and five more were injured. Three of the terrorists blew themselves up when they were confronted. Three escaped but were later captured after an attack on a mission hospital. During the hearing they confessed that they had intended to kill all 150 children. They had rented an apartment near the school and had been observing the school for three months. They knew exactly when the children had their break and where they stayed. Their plan was to attack at exactly the time when the children had their break and were outside in large numbers. They had grenades and Kalashnikovs with them. They wanted to throw the grenades and then mow down any surviving students with the Kalashnikovs.

And then one miracle after another happened. It's impossible to have so many coincidences at once. One classroom stood on its own just beyond the entrance. When the teacher heard the first shots at the watchmen, he recognized it as an attack, and with great presence of mind, fled with his students to a school building situated higher up. When the first terrorists stormed through the entrance, they had already disappeared around the corner. Another class was supposed to have their sports lesson on the basketball court, which would have been directly in the terrorists' field of vision from the entrance area. But no, they had switched their class to the multipurpose hall inside the church building. Instead of playing basketball, they were watching a film. Had they been playing outside, the terrorists would have noticed the noise, but as it was, they rushed on past.

Besides the sports students, there were other classes being held there, as well as some in offices, including the school principal.

As it was, they ran past onto the upper level of the property, where another school building was situated, as well as the dining hall and the quadrangle. From the quad one can see into several classrooms. Fortunately they couldn't see any students as they were all hidden under their desks. The terrorists had expected that the quad would be full of students having their break. For some reason or other, the break times had been changed a short time earlier, with the result that the students were already back in class. Frustrated not to have encountered any students, the terrorists fired random shots into one of the buildings. Meantime the police from a nearby garrison had become aware of the noise and were approaching, whereupon the terrorists fled over the school fence. However on their way to the fence they caught sight of three Pakistani school staff who had hidden behind a building; they were shot dead. Three of the terrorists then killed themselves with grenades and the remaining three were later caught by the police.

Daniel Taubmann: I had only been in the school for one week. The attack was on Monday, and on the previous Saturday we played football outside. The football field was outside the school and as I was looking in the direction of the school, I saw clouds like a gigantic hand over the building. I sensed then how God was saying to me, *Daniel, I am protecting you. I am with you and all*

the others. When the attack happened, we were just having a chemistry class. I heard something like fireworks. I thought it was balloons bursting. But others understood immediately what was going on. Then I felt queasy. *This sort of thing only happens in America, not with us.*

Can this be true? I thought. We were told to crouch down very close to the wall. Far away from the windows. When I think back on it, I know that I was afraid. Others really panicked. We held one another's hands and prayed quietly. But it wasn't traumatizing for me. There was, of course, a lot of fear in the situation. We kept hoping that no one would come up the stairs and force their way into our room. It was really dreadful, but then somehow it was over. We were able to leave and were sent to the multipurpose hall. When I saw a policeman shooting, that was really the worst moment for me. Afterwards, you're hypersensitive to loud noise. When you hear explosions, you're startled and think something awful is about to happen. For a long time afterwards I would be startled. People did die during the attack, but I didn't know them personally. The traces of blood and the dead bodies were cleared away quickly. I didn't see them. We were also well cared for afterwards and were able to talk a lot about it, so I haven't suffered any psychological harm.

INVOLVEMENT IN PAKISTAN INCREASES

While the staff of other aid organizations left Pakistan in a state of shock and many NGOs closed their projects down, Shelter Now not only maintained its commitments in Pakistan but also expanded them. Georg, who had almost lost his son, did not want to give up. On the return trip to Afghanistan, he traveled via Peshawar and met up with the staff there. He related to them what had happened and they discussed how things in Pakistan should proceed. Until then, Shelter Now had only a mandate to work among Afghan refugees in Pakistan.

But Georg had the vision to carry out development projects also for poor and needy Pakistani people as well. Therefore they decided to apply for registration to do this—in spite of the present dangerous situation. A few years later it was evident how wise this planning was.

Georg Taubmann: I thought I was crazy and hardly dared say it. We had just gone through this drama and I still had the desire to carry out development work in Pakistan among the poor and needy. But I found open ears among our colleagues, and we applied to the authorities for a new registration of Shelter Now, with the aim of carrying out general and emergency aid.

The application took time to be carried through. But when a devastating earthquake struck North Pakistan in 2005, Shelter Now was among the first of the aid agencies to distribute relief in the affected areas. In the region which was so badly destroyed they rebuilt 25 schools. In 2010, when the population was affected by a huge flood disaster, Shelter Now was able to offer extensive help. Shelter Now has a good reputation, not only due to its decade-long refugee relief for Afghans in northern Pakistan, but also because of the quick disaster aid and relief projects among Pakistanis.

MARIANNE WITH THE BOYS IN GERMANY

After Daniel and Benjamin had finished their schooling in Chiang Mai in 2004, the family decided that Marianne should move with the two boys to Sulzbach-Rosenberg in South Germany, to Georg's parents' house, where the grandparents lived.

Georg came twice a year to Germany, in summer and at Christmas, and Marianne flew two times a year to Kabul, for two to three weeks each time. They didn't want to leave the boys alone for a longer period in Germany. In this way, Marianne and Georg could see each other at least four times a year, and Marianne could keep up contact with their colleagues in Kabul.

Initially they didn't know how many years this traveling to and fro between the continents would last, but it was important that the boys got used to living in Germany and could stand on their own feet.

Marianne Taubmann: For me it was quite a shock, a massive change, to be in Germany without Georg. I had spent almost twenty years by his side in Asia.

Overseas we lived in a team who met often, undertook and worked lots together— and then suddenly you're here alone with two sons, one of whom was doing a two-year theological training and the other undertaking a practical course with his uncle. I was more or less thrown on my own resources, together with Georg's parents. Both required help and support in the house. They passed on increasing responsibility to me as far as the house was concerned, as well as financial decisions.

However I was able to go every day to the team meetings of a partner organization in a neighboring town, which was very important for me. Without this daily fellowship, when we also prayed with each other, getting used to living in Germany would simply have been too difficult. I found the orientation to German culture, and the separation from Georg and Daniel and my many friends extremely difficult.

INTERVIEW WITH DANIEL AND BENJAMIN TAUBMANN

When Georg was taken captive, his two sons, Daniel and Benjamin, were 16 and 14 years old. Suddenly the situation for the family and for all the other foreign staff of Shelter Now was extremely threatening. A friendly Talib searches out Marianne at home and informs her that Georg has been captured and that both she and the boys are in danger. He offers to take them to his house and to protect them. But Marianne makes the decision to flee the following morning by road to Pakistan. She and the boys quickly burn and hide all the things which could be considered offensive by the Religious Police, and mementos which they love— photos, holiday souvenirs and dearly loved music CDs. Despite a premium on space, Marianne allows the boys to take their beloved guinea pigs.

Daniel Taubmann, 16 years old

Benjamin Taubmann, 14 years old

Eberhard: How did you feel when your father was in prison and you fled first to Pakistan and then returned to Germany?

Daniel: I was probably naive and so didn't take the situation too seriously. I simply trusted that Papa would come back. We prayed for him, and Mama and the other colleagues were there for us. We were always with friends going somewhere. That was important. When we later arrived in Germany, Gran and Grandpa were there and again there were friends. I always felt well cared for, so I was emotionally fine.

Benjamin: I think it was the same for me. We'd known similar dangerous situations and they always worked out okay. Because lots of people were around and we had prayed as a fellowship, I felt safe and secure. After Papa's arrest we were about a month in Pakistan, where we lived with very close friends. Every day we could hang around and play with our friends. Sometimes I tried to paint a picture of what it would be like if something bad happened to Papa, but I couldn't imagine it.

Eberhard: Did the Taliban not pose a threat to you?

Daniel: For us, the Taliban weren't a threat. We knew that Papa had good contacts with some of them. I also picked up how, on the evening Papa was arrested, a Talib came by and reported it to Mama and offered to protect us. Mama was able to pack something for Papa in prison and give it to him. I had a few sweets which I put in as well. We knew nice, helpful Taliban, so on the whole they didn't pose a threat to us.

Benjamin: Personally we didn't have any bad experiences with the Taliban, though we would have had with Al Qaeda supporters. One time they pursued us when we were out in the car with Papa. Or whenever we went to a restaurant, we were stared at really maliciously by the foreign terrorists. We felt there are wicked people and there are good people, and we knew more of the good. The really bad things like whipping and executions, or hands being chopped off … we didn't witness that. We did of course hear about it, but have never seen it ourselves.

Eberhard: I can imagine some readers asking themselves: how can one bring up children in such a dangerous land? How did you experience the general danger?

Daniel: For us, everyday life was just normal. We knew there are certain things one can do and some which one absolutely cannot. For me it was no restriction. The other overseas children weren't on the street either, playing around. Everyone stayed in their own grounds.

Benjamin: For a start, we didn't always really recognize the danger, and as well, we trusted our parents and God. There were situations where we saw it as more of an adventure. I am very thankful that our parents made the decision to take us with them! In many respects it was most enriching.

Shortly before Papa's arrest we did notice that there was somehow tension in the air. We picked up how Mama and Papa were hiding things. I found that more exciting than threatening. Hiding things, that was really cool, to find a good hiding place and put the things in it. We hid some things so well that we never found them again. That was exciting. And burning something? Now that was great fun!

Eberhard: Tell me what your day-to-day life was like. In Kabul you two had home schooling.

Daniel: We got up in the morning about 7 o'clock, had breakfast and tried to be back in our room by eight; that was also our classroom. Then Silke came. We had our material from the German distance-learning program, which we worked through. Silke was there and helped to get us going.

Benjamin: As Dani had already mentioned, we had lessons from 8 am till 1:30 pm. After that we either met friends or busied ourselves elsewhere.

Daniel: The afternoon was our own. We did our homework and studied. We had really good friends—those whom we already knew from Pakistan and then new ones who we got to know in Kabul. Except that meeting up with them wasn't always easy, as for that we needed a driver. We couldn't just get on to a public bus; we always needed a driver. I think during the Taliban period we were able to meet our friends once a week.

Benjamin: Once a week we were also at the German Tennis Club. The owner, who spoke perfect German, taught us how to play tennis. Silke did a lot with us too. Once a week we worked creatively with pottery. We built a kiln ourselves and fired things in it. Off and on we were also in the office. But often we were just doing things in the garden, playing there, building a fire, collecting ammunition or looking after our guinea pigs.

Eberhard: When you look back, did you find it boring?

Daniel: It was never boring; it was wonderful and exciting. We were able to do things which German children can't do. I can remember how we pulled bullets out of the wall of the house and collected them. Or we built tremendous fires, with plastic or grass and damp foliage. That produced glorious colors and a powerful stink.

Eberhard: Then came the spring of 2002, and you went back as a family to Pakistan and then to Kabul again. How did that happen? Did your parents talk it over with you?

Benjamin: We couldn't wait to go back. I don't remember that they asked us. For me it was clear that we should go back as soon as possible. There was no other alternative. Germany was a stopover for me, but not a country in which I wanted to live long term.

Eberhard: You're not like some of those kids who just reluctantly follow their parents, then?

Daniel: No, no way! We were right behind them. It would have been awful to have stayed in Germany. We're a family and our home was over there. When we first came back to Pakistan, we stayed with friends. That was familiar … a familiar environment. I felt at home right away. And then we were off to Kabul. We were so happy to meet the people again.

Benjamin: It was thrilling to go back. Our house had of course been ransacked and it was a total mess. But it was exciting to sort through everything and to look for our treasures in the old hiding places. That was just fantastic! Another reason to look forward to our return was that the team members were like an extended family to me. We used to meet every Friday evening. I just loved the fellowship.

Eberhard: After the attack on the boarding school in Pakistan, you both went to school for a while in Chiang Mai in Thailand, finished school there and then went back to Germany with your mother. That was probably the longest period for you in Germany? What was it like settling in?

Daniel: When we were on home leave, we used to visit Gran and Grandpa and friends. We travelled around a lot, always for such a short time that we didn't have to go to school. There were two main places where we stayed, Braunschweig and then Bavaria. We had finished school in Thailand fortunately, so we didn't have to go to school in Germany.

That was my big worry, having to go to school in Germany. I was spared that, thank goodness. Subconsciously I envisaged films in which there were always outsiders. I identified with them and was afraid of being mobbed. So I was happy that we never had to go to a German school. We were able to cover everything through distance learning in German and happily that was all finally recognized in Germany.

Benjamin: Coming back to Germany naturally had its advantages and disadvantages. I was very happy to be living at last near my best friends in Germany. On the other hand it was very hard to get used to German culture and the pace of life.

Eberhard: When you think back to your childhood, what were the best experiences or what are your best memories?

Benjamin: Firstly, the good and deep relationships with my friends, like the Gilmores and others. Secondly, we had the freedom to mess with dynamite and build rockets. I have lots of happy memories of the UN Club and the American Club.

Daniel: We had very many friends, good friendships. We were outside a lot, and I well remember the times together with friends. Also the spiritual life together in the team was superb. As children we felt completely accepted. The praise times were always brilliant. During prayer times of course we sometimes switched off, but we were always switched on again during the songs. Life in Kabul was always associated with friendships, we never felt isolated.

Eberhard: When you think back, what were the most unpleasant, and what the saddest experiences?

Daniel: I regret now that I didn't appreciate and learn the language. I had too little contact with Afghan children. I'd do it differently today. But then I didn't see it like that. I was happy not to have to learn more.

Benjamin: When Daniel went to boarding school, for me, that was the saddest. I still remember the time when we visited you in Thailand and then had to say goodbye. How Mama and I got into the bus, and Dani stood there and waved till the bus could no longer be seen in the distance.

Daniel: That was really awful. I cried the whole day. Or also when I went to the big school in Pakistan. I had such pains in my tummy and was just so frightened that I was sick before class. Or on my 17th birthday in Chiang Mai when my parents tried to call me and the connection didn't work. That was really frustrating. Sometimes I was quite lonely, there in Thailand. Simply because I wasn't used to being away from my parents and Benni.

Benjamin: Anyway we are very thankful for our childhood and teenage years in Pakistan and Afghanistan. In comparison with Germany it was almost Paradise.

GEORG ALONE IN KABUL—YEARS OF EXTENSIVE REBUILDING

From 2004 to 2008, Georg lives alone in Kabul and leads the international team for Afghanistan. He and Marianne oscillate between Afghanistan and Germany, to at least have some family life.

These will be years of extensive rebuilding of many aid projects. But also years in which the security situation dramatically intensifies, not just for Shelter Now but for all relief agencies. The influence and the power of the Taliban increase and are soon manifested in bloody attacks every week. Increasingly, aid organizations are concerned for the safety of their staff and leave the country.

Shelter Now is one of the few organizations which not only do not give up, but constantly expand.

Georg Taubmann: Even if I was sorry about Marianne and the two boys, I knew I had to stay. So many new colleagues from all over the world were arriving and daily life in Kabul was becoming ever more dangerous. I had only a few colleagues on the team who had been there longer, who were well aware of the security situation and could lead the new people.

During these years the team grew to about 30 foreign staff, and according to the various projects which were running, there were about another 100 to 150 Afghan workers. The foreign staff came from up to 15 different countries. That resulted in a variegated troop. The various gifts, cultural roots and habits had to be acknowledged and encouraged.

Shelter Now's work expanded. New projects kept being added, but the danger intensified year by year. The first project in Shamalie, "Villages of Hope," was running well. A new team went to Herat, another was formed in the northeastern part of Afghanistan. New projects were begun, many of which provided drinking water—by sinking boreholes, installing wells and piping drinking water from sources in the mountains down to the villages. Furthermore, Shelter Now repaired lots of irrigation plants, also called *kareeze*.

In 2007, Shelter Now began a project with a nomadic people group, the Kuchies. During the Taliban period they were persecuted and the majority of their livestock, mostly sheep, died in the devastating five-year drought. Their means of livelihood was gone.

Kuchi families received microcredit to buy five ewes, and a ram for every three families. After one year, the credit was repaid and given to new families. In this way, after five years, they had accumulated a herd of 50 animals, which could sustain a whole family.

A Kuchi boy with his young camel

The Orchard Training project that the Herat team set up was called "Trees of Hope", as the people in Herat province really needed new hope. The most severe winter in living memory had hit this area of Afghanistan especially hard and taken many lives.

Many animals had frozen to death. A considerable number of fruit trees, especially pomegranates, did not survive the frost. With that, their means of livelihood was ruined—or, indeed, destroyed. Together with a Forestry School in Holland and the support of the Dutch Government, new fruit trees were planted in the provinces of Herat, Kabul and Badakshan, covering an area of approximately 200,000 square meters. The goal of this project however was not just the cultiva-

The young fruit trees are planted with enthusiasm and joy

tion of resistant types of fruit, but 50 fruit tree specialists were simultaneously being trained. They can now pass on their specialist knowledge to other regions.

"Saffron instead of Opium" was the name of another new project. Saffron, the most expensive spice in the world, helps farmers in Afghanistan to build up a new livelihood.

Farmers with the saffron harvest

Farmers from Herat Province were given saffron bulbs, fertilizer and the requisite know-how in saffron production. They paid no money up front, but instead, for the following four years they give a quarter of their saffron harvest to Shelter Now.

After five years the bulbs have increased four- or five-fold. The farmers dig them up and give half of them to Shelter Now, and so new projects are begun with other farmers. The other half is retained by the farmers, the bulbs are planted in new fields, and a further cycle of saffron growing begins. From now on they keep 100% of the harvest and thus can earn more than in the illegal cultivation of opium.

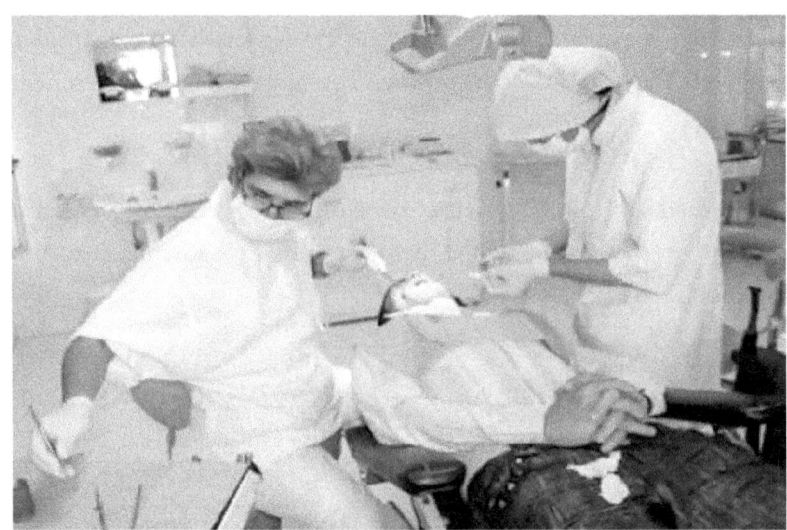
Dental Clinic

In West Afghanistan a dental clinic has been set up. It is seen as the most modern of its kind in the whole country. It is led by a German-Iranian dentist. She is a blessing to the population there; up to 70 patients a day seek her help. She also trains Afghan dentists and dental assistants. In the schools regular check-ups are carried out and dental care packs are distributed to the children.

In Kabul a beauty salon for women was set up. Shelter Now also took over a primary school there. In the northeast they supported an orphanage and offered vocational training to the orphans. In a center for the deaf, they learn sign language and receive a school education and vocational training.

The two cement works in Khost and Kandahar are still producing concrete roofing material and also linings for wells. All in all, many projects came into being during these years, which in subsequent years ran increasingly independently and made an enormous contribution to the reconstruction in these areas or regions.

ATTACKS ON GEORG

At the beginning of 2008, Shelter Now received information from the American State Department that an attack on Georg was planned. Georg was requested to come to the American Embassy. He set off with an American colleague. The official at the Embassy informed him with a somber face that they had information that the Taliban wanted to take Georg captive again.

"How reliable is this information?" Georg enquired.

"Absolutely reliable, and your life is in great danger," was the response. "You need to be very careful. It would be best if you left the country immediately."

About a week later Georg received a call from the German Embassy with the same warning, likewise from the Afghan Secret Service. In February and March Georg survived two attempts to kidnap him.

Georg Taubmann: One night when I was driving home, a speeding jeep overtook me and cut in front of me. It stopped in front of my Pajero and tried to make me brake. I nearly drove into the side of the jeep and had to come to a halt. I was furious! *How can anyone drive so idiotically?* I thought. It didn't strike me what was going on. Only when several men jumped out of the jeep and ran towards me did I realize the seriousness of the situation. Fortunately the engine was still running. I quickly put it into first gear, swerved to the side and raced past the people and the vehicle in front. Fortunately the road was wide enough for this overtaking manoeuvre. I raced home like a madman. My pulse racing, I flew through the gate into the security of our place. I was so agitated I couldn't sleep the whole night. *Man, that was close*, I kept thinking. "Thank you, Lord, that I escaped."

Some weeks later I was driving home from the office with Marianne. She was visiting from Germany. It was already dark. I had to slow down at a speedbump and drive slowly over it. At that moment a man stepped out of the darkness and shone a bright light into the car, straight into my face. When he recognized me, he quickly switched off the flashlight. I suspected there was something up. Just then a vehicle with darkened windows and headlights on full beam came racing up behind me.

Fortunately I was right at the crossroads leading to the street where our house was. I turned off quickly, but the vehicle followed doggedly. Diagonally opposite our house there is an Indian hospital, which always has armed guards posted at the entrance. When the pursuers saw the men with Kalashnikovs, they reversed and raced backwards out of the street, their tires screeching.

These kidnap attempts profoundly shocked Georg. He limited his car journeys and visits and kept taking different routes in order to prevent an attack. In the team, they talked about these dangerous assaults. Naturally the question arose as to whether Georg should leave Afghanistan for the sake of his safety. But in a few months, in July 2008, a change in leadership was planned. Georg was to open an international office in Germany; that had already been arranged by the Board. The new leader however was unable to come before July. Georg had the impression that, if he would slip away before the leadership transfer, it would not be good for either the team or the work as a whole. Therefore he wanted to stay till the handover.

> For some considerable time the Board had been concerned to release Georg from leadership responsibilities in Afghanistan for an international, worldwide role. At an important meeting in 2007 in Kabul, one of the international leaders, whose advice was highly respected, expressed this opinion: "Georg, you must get away from the daily routines in Kabul. It is time to hand over the work to someone else. You should build up an international office and an international service, so that the work can continue to grow. If you don't get away from here, then our organizations and the work cannot grow." At first Georg thought of settling in another area of the city or in Dubai or maybe in England. Eventually they chose Sulzbach-Rosenberg in South Germany. Finally Georg could live with his family again, and Marianne could work in the office.

SHELTER NOW INTERNATIONAL OFFICE IN GERMANY

Everything went well. There were no renewed kidnap attempts. In July 2008, Georg was able to travel to Germany, in order to set up the international office in Sulzbach-Rosenberg, his home place in South Germany. A few streets away from their house they found suitable office space, which they furnished.

Marianne was happy to have Georg at home with her again and to be working with him in the new office. Daniel was studying Agriculture and Benjamin was doing his National Service in an orphanage.

In the ensuing period, Georg established connections with other organizations: in England, Northern Ireland, Holland, Finland, the Czech Republic, Romania, Norway, Sweden, Austria, Belgium, the Ukraine and also in Brazil, Korea, the USA, Argentina, Australia, the Philippines and Tajikistan. In some of these countries new Shelter Now offices were opened (Holland, England and Australia), and other organisations in the above countries supported Shelter Now with personnel and/or finance.

Through Georg's worldwide speaking tours new personnel were drawn in, which previously would not have been possible. Everywhere Georg went and gave talks, people were mobilized. Meanwhile workers came from Finland, the Czech Republic, Romania, Australia, Uruguay, Argentina, Brazil, El Salvador, from the Philippines—from up to 20 different countries.

All applicants who are interested in working for Shelter Now make contact with the International office and are given preparation there for the tasks relevant to the country in which they want to work. Finally, they attend a three- or four-week preparation course led by Shelter Now, before they go to their place of operation.

THE YEARS 2008-2018

New Projects

The tried and tested projects are expanded during these years and new ones added. After long negotiations with the village elders, in 2009, a micro-credit project for buying a cow was introduced in one of the "Villages of Hope." In the first year 27 cows were offered for sale. When the money was paid back after 12 months, it was invested in the next families, so that more families became proud owners of a cow. Some of the calves had already been sold and in this way the whole village could be provided for. As the money keeps being reinvested, yet more villages are provided with cows. Guarantors for the repayment of the small credit sums are a "Cow Committee" chosen by the village elders themselves. The committee works in an honorary capacity, they seek out the most needy and most reliable families.

A villager—happy with his newly acquired cow

Education, especially for girls, has always been a matter of great concern for Shelter Now. There are sponsorships for pupils and more and more projects have been started. For example, a new Learning Center in Kabul which started in 2018. It resembles the well-known Montessori teaching method in Europe. Part of the method of instruction requires the mothers of the children to be involved.

They are to be present, as far as possible, with the three-to five-year-olds and learn with them through play. Also, culturally determined negative attitudes (problems to do with equal rights, violence, etc.) are to be "unlearned" and replaced with positive attitudes (peaceful conflict resolution).

Education for girls is especially close to SN's heart

In Afghanistan, they say, "Honey is medicine," and honey is extremely popular and correspondingly expensive. Two local colleagues were won over by a pilot project, and one of them especially developed a knack for working with the flying insects. Under the leadership of a qualified expert he breeds bees very successfully and produces good honey. He has now gained so much experience that he is going to head up a bee project.

A beekeeper at work

In 2014 they began with ten families. These families did possess some land on which they grew vegetables for their own use but it was insufficient to sustain the family. Each of these families first received two beehives and the necessary training and equipment; later the number of beehives was increased to five. They had to learn how to handle the bees properly, so that they produced a good amount of honey. The proper processing and packing of the honey also required training, and last but not least, marketing. After six months the families should be functioning independently, though they would receive further technical support and advice as required.

In 2016 Shelter Now was able to open a second dental clinic in Herat. The first Shelter Now dental clinic was handed over to the 212
Afghan Government in May 2014. As with the first clinic, Shelter Now works medically and hygienically according to European standards.

What is new in the present clinic is cooperation with the University; and male and female students are offered a practical educa-tion. At the heart of the new set up is the School Dentist programme. As has been the case in Europe for decades, boys and girls are examined, treated and trained in oral hygiene. In total approximately 11,000 people have been direct beneficiaries of the scheme.

The free treatment was concentrated primarily on women and children, who make up about 70 per cent of the patients. Ten per cent were children with special needs, orphans or street children, who otherwise would have had no chance of dental treatment. In Afghanistan up till now less there is less than one dentist per 20,000 of the population (in Germany: 16 per 20,000).

70% of the patients are women and children

Work under increasingly dangerous conditions

During this period, Georg only visits Kabul—still, he comes two or three times a year. He is an outside observer and adviser. The security situation for all relief agencies is worsening from year to year. During the course of these years, of the foreigners whom Georg has known personally, more than 30 have been killed.

For security reasons more and more aid organizations have withdrawn from Afghanistan. Large organizations which employed over 100 staff in 2002, have seen many of their staff leave the country. Many offices are shut. Presently only very few organizations are on the ground. Shelter Now staff have been threatened

> The increase in the influence of the Taliban can be well illustrated from the trunk roads into and out of Kabul. From Kabul the roads radiate out in all directions.
>
> One main road goes North in the direction of Mazar–i-Sharif, the other to the West to Herat. In the south it goes to Kandahar, in the southeast to Khost, and in the east to Pakistan. In 2002 all roads could be travelled without danger. And then suddenly it was no longer possible to travel to Kandahar. It was in 2003 that the Taliban wanted to conquer this city as its headquarters. Then it became dangerous to drive on the road to Khost. Then towards Pakistan and eventually the road to Mazar–i-Sharif/Kunduz became partially controlled by the Taliban.
>
> From 2015 after the withdrawal of the ISAF, all roads to and from Kabul were dangerous.

a number of times. There are several attacks near their office. Yet they stay and not only maintain their number of staff, but expand their enterprises.

Georg Taubmann: On each visit I could observe that the security situation had become worse. Among the terror victims were more and more overseas workers. In Kabul there is hardly a restaurant left which foreigners like to go to. A number of restaurants have been victims of an attack. Even the large hotels are no longer safe.

A long-time friend and partner of ours, Brigitte Weiler, who had been engaged in aid projects for children in Afghanistan for almost 30 years and

Brigitte Weiler with some of the girls she cared for

also supported some of ours, was on the way to Kabul. Before her flight she called me from Stuttgart airport. "Georg, please pray with me." She was worried about her safety.

While she normally stayed with friends or in simple guesthouses, this time she had chosen the Intercontinental in Kabul. The hotel is regarded as one of the best protected in the Afghan capital. But it was this hotel which was attacked by radical Islamic Taliban on the night of January 20-21, 2018. Eyewitnesses reported to me that six terrorists specifically targeted foreigners. The assault lasted twelve hours. Then the attackers were dead—and also 24 guests and staff of the hotel, among them 14 foreigners. Some of our colleagues had to identify Brigitte's body. They were extremely upset.

Marianne and I and two Shelter Now colleagues were at Brigitte's funeral. It was a very sad, moving time. Brigitte had such a love for Afghanistan. She paid a heavy price for this love—she paid with her life. Completing her current projects lies close to our hearts.

There are various reasons for the Taliban gaining strength. At the end of 2001 they had to withdraw, defeated, mainly to Pakistan. In 2002 they gathered their forces but maintained a low profile. But by 2003 they reappeared with their first attacks on the Afghan security forces, the ISAF, and on foreign troops. A contributory factor was the Iraq War, also known as the Third Gulf War. The Americans, who had deployed the most troops within the ISAF in Afghanistan, diverted their attention and troops more intensively on Iraq. That must have encouraged the Taliban towards more focused terror involvement, because their influence and attacks now intensified considerably.

A further event which led to the strengthening of the Taliban was the withdrawal of the ISAF from Afghanistan at the end of 2014. From January 1, 2015, around 12,000 NATO soldiers were supposed to train, advise and support the Afghan security forces, but without any longer being involved militarily themselves. The preceding years, however, were simply not long enough to instruct the Afghan forces and police to a sufficiently high level, so that they could take over the security measures independently. The Taliban took advantage of this to carry out even more targeted attacks and take over certain areas.

> The Iraq war or Third Gulf War was a military invasion of Iraq by the USA, Great Britain and a "Coalition of the Willing." It began on March 20, 2003, with the bombardment of selected targets in Baghdad and led to the capitulation of the city and the downfall of Iraqi President Saddam Hussein. On May 1, 2003, President George W. Bush declared victory and the end of the war.

Georg Taubmann: I myself witnessed how the withdrawal of the ISAF created absolute dismay among the population and caused panic among many. No one could envisage how they could defend themselves against the Taliban when the troops were no longer there. It was not only soldiers who were withdrawn, but also tanks, helicopters and equipment. After the Americans announced their withdrawal, other countries too did not wish to remain.

Not only were large sections of the population horrified, the international relief agencies too became uncomfortable. Year by year they were experiencing an increasing number of attacks which were now being carried out specifically on foreigners. How could their protection be assured after the departure of the ISAF? The departure of the ISAF produced a renewed withdrawal of foreign relief organizations. Workers no longer dared to stay in the country. Some of the organizations turned to us and offered us their projects. In individual cases we were able to accept. Financial aid also dwindled. Interest in Afghanistan disappeared. The violent clashes had been going on for so many years that many supporters became weary.

Shelter Now too became increasingly aware of threats from the Taliban. To witness the attacks on restaurants, hotels, hospitals and foreign installations gnaws away at one's nerves. There were some weeks when they could only go from their homes to their offices and back. Maybe go shopping briefly, but visiting friends in another part of the city, for example, was inadvisable. It was particularly oppressive when friends or colleagues in organizations close to us lost their lives in the attacks. In 2010 an eight-man medical team, some of them friends of ours, were murdered by the Taliban in the mountains in the north of Afghanistan. That shattered all of us. Or the death of Werner Groenewald and his two teenage children who were murdered on Nov. 29th, 2014, in the guesthouse where they lived in Kabul, along with two Afghans. Werner was Director of the aid organization Partnership in Academics and Development (PAD) and was a friend of Georg.

Then on January 20st of 2018, Brigitte Weiler, a close friend of Georg and Marianne, was killed by the Taliban in the Intercontinental. It makes one think about one's own life and future. Individuals in Shelter Now also left the country.

In the implementation and care of their projects, the Shelter Now workers feel increasingly restricted. At present, for security reasons, they can no longer travel to Shamalie, where they began with the Villages of Hope plan in 2002 and also set up a concrete girder factory, although it is only 40 minutes away by car.

Production has had to be closed down. The influence and the power of the Taliban are too great.

Presently around 10 foreign colleagues work in Kabul; they deal with the necessary administrative tasks for the projects and for member care, financial administration and the costly reports for the government and donor organizations.

In 2015, under pressure from the police, they had to transform their office building almost into a "fortress." The walls around the complex were heightened, barbed wire was rolled out along the top and stronger steel doors added. Now entrance to the property is only possible through a double-door system. In the office itself a safe-room was built in with windows of special glass and a reinforced steel door, as well as an escape route to the neighboring plot.

Experts state that, in the event of an attack, these security measures afford the escapees three minutes extra time to flee or to reach safety.

Recently the Save the Children organization was attacked in Jalalabad. As per their usual procedure, a Talib blew himself up at the entrance so that the other terrorists could force their way into the building. The staff were able to escape into their safe-room and were freed by the police. It was a great miracle that no one was harmed.

The walls around the office building were heightened and topped with barbed wire

Benjamin Taubmann: In 2017, after a five-year break, I visited Kabul again with my wife Lisa. For Lisa it was her first time. I was astonished how much the city had changed, even in a positive sense. There are so many new roads and buildings that I found it difficult find my way around in unfamiliar surroundings.

I found the security arrangements alienating and threatening. Houses which looked like fortresses, road checks and concrete structures everywhere which had to be circumvented. When you drove along some streets, you saw mostly high concrete walls with barbed wire. It's like as if you were driving along beside a prison wall in Germany. Except that it's not just occasional, but whole processions of streets look like that. We tried to find our old house. I'd have loved to show it to Lisa. But it wasn't possible. The whole street was blocked off, everywhere there were soldiers, check-posts and concrete boulders.

We weren't allowed just to drive around at all, to go sightseeing or to visit friends. I don't remember it like that before. There was a certain tension in the atmosphere, one was always on the look-out.

We then went North and had a look at the projects. There we were able to breathe again. The security situation is much better there and we were able to freely go for walks.

Georg Taubmann: Outside of Kabul, in the countryside near Herat or Mazar-i-Sharif, it is easier to implement projects. The security situation is better there, although one must be careful when traveling. Villages which are free of Taliban influence today can be occupied by them a week later. One has always got to be watchful.

Fortunately, our Afghan colleagues are very responsible and independent. The majority of the projects are led by them.

From time to time we have to visit them, of course, and see if everything is being done properly. We keep up relationships with the donors, draw up the accounts and write the reports. When the situation is very dangerous, we don't have to go to the projects. Right from our time in Pakistan we were always careful to see that we trained our local colleagues to work independently. Otherwise we couldn't have maintained our concrete girder factories.

At this point I would like to emphasize strongly that the work of Shelter Now was carried on only because devoted people worked with great commitment and risked their lives—often under huge challenges, facing great danger and sacrifice. During this time many foreigners from other relief agencies were killed, some of them friends of ours and of our colleagues. We lost a dear and very committed young colleague, who was shot by Islamic fanatics, 28-year-old Sajid, who leaves behind a wife and young daughter.

Several governments have come and gone in Afghanistan, but we have managed to work with each of them and to build up and maintain many projects. We are deeply grateful to all colleagues for their commitment, which has made it possible to do everything that has been reported in this book. For that we are not only thankful to the overseas team, but above all to our local colleagues. "Thank you for your cooperation, dependability and also loyalty to Shelter Now! Without you we could never have done this work." They have been exposed to great danger, because many of them work in areas that are very dangerous.

When we eight Shelter Now staff were arrested, 16 of our local colleagues were also thrown in prison, and they had similar awful experiences. We will never forget their sacrifices. Through a great miracle they also were set free unharmed, and many worked with us again later.

I also want to express my very personal thanks to my friend of many years, Udo Stolte and his wife Sieglinde. Udo visited us often in Pakistan and in Afghanistan and was often on the road with me, also in dangerous areas. He too has a great love for this people and their land. Udo has built up our organization in Germany, and through his help we have been able to carry out many projects in Afghanistan.

Without the strong support of my wife, Marianne, I would never have been able to carry on the work. She has stood by me in all the dangers and huge challenges, has always encouraged me and was prepared, each time our organization or we personally were under attack or threat, to begin again with me and to go on. *Return to Kabul* is our joint story. Our two sons were born in Pakistan and grew up there and in Afghanistan. I am always thankful to have had her with me. Marianne was always a model mother and has fulfilled her role in an amazing way. Even today the boys love to think back on this time, in spite of all they missed out on.

Also I am very thankful to my sons Daniel and Benjamin, who went with us through good and difficult and very challenging times and never complained about it but always supported us in our work. They often had to live a simple life with a lot of restrictions, especially when we lived in Afghanistan under the Taliban regime, but were always content with what they had.

I also want to express my very personal thanks to the founder of our organization, Douglas Layton, and to Greg and Shelvi Gilmore, who faithfully worked with us for many years and especially helped us very much in rebuilding SNI after the destruction of SNI in 1990 and in 2002. Their three children have become very close friends of Daniel and Benjamin.

I have met few people with such a deep love for the Afghan people as David and Julie Leatherberry, and they served them for many years in Pakistan and Afghanistan and other countries with great dedication. It has been a great encouragement for us to work with them for many years together in SNI.

Without Len and Diane Stitt it would have been difficult to build up SNI in Afghanistan during the Taliban regime and after we returned to Kabul in 2002 we had to rebuild our organization from scratch and they had a very significant part in that.

There are many committed, caring and very hard-working men and women, foreigners who came from many different countries and our faithful staff members from Afghanistan and Pakistan, who labored with us in Pakistan and Afghanistan with great dedication. If we would mention all of them here it would fill a many pages of this book. They made it possible that we were able to help so many tens of thousands of Afghans over so many years in very significant ways.

Above all, we would like to thank our Lord Jesus, whom we follow. He is our great example; he gave us strength in all the challenging situations and preserved us. Only through His help were we able to gather new courage and keep doing this work!

There is at present no nation of people who have suffered as much as the Afghans. Since 1979, war has been raging in this land, which was already one of the poorest on earth. It has been 40 years during which the people have known only waves of violence, death and destruction. We admire the

Afghan people deeply. Those who have remained in the country simply continue where most human beings would have given up. In spite of the terror and the suffering, many have not lost the courage to face life and the hope that one day there will be peace.

What comforts people in need and what they require is for others to stand by them.

Many came when the Taliban were overthrown, but most have left them on their own again. We want to continue to stand by them and with God's help see that their hope for the country does not get lost; together with them we want to rebuild their land.

We believe with them that it will not take long till peace reigns again in Afghanistan. At the moment that does not look likely, and the conflict has become worse. The Taliban again control large areas of the country. But we also know that the night is darkest just before the dawn. May it be so in Afghanistan and may the sun rise soon over this land.

35 Years of Shelter Now International— From Its Exciting Beginnings Until Today

THE YEARS 1979-1989

Civil Wars and Floods of Refugees

In 1979 news appeared in the world's media that the Soviet Union and its Allies had marched into Afghanistan. They interfered in the internal Afghan civil conflict, deposed the reigning President, and installed an Afghan Communist government. As Afghanistan is a strongly conservative Islamic country, there was soon armed conflict. For many Afghans, living under a Communist regime was intolerable.

The resistance battles were carried out with the support of the mujahideen (those who wage a "holy war"). Thus the movement of refugees began over the mountains to Pakistan. At first in their thousands, then in their tens of thousands, then hundreds of thousands. All were accommodated in camps around Peshawar, as well as in the northwest, known at that time as the North West Frontier Province.

1979

The Soviet Union and it's allies invade Afghanistan with the Red Army. The religious leaders (mujahideen) call for a "Holy War" against the Soviet occupiers and the government in Kabul. Massive refugee movements begin across the mountains into North Pakistan.

1982

During a three-and-a-half month work experience in India, Georg Taubmann pays a visit to his friends in Pakistan. Together they visited some of the refugee camps there in the country. He is shocked at the catastrophic conditions in the camps. Negotiations are begun with the Pakistan Government to grant permission for a humanitarian organization for Afghan refugees. In 1982 registration is applied for and it is granted one year later.

1983

In January, in an adventuresome trip, Georg and three friends transport some old trucks by road to the refugee camps in Pakistan. Shelter Now opens an office in the Pakistani border town Peshawar. Primary aim is to erect low cost houses for the refugees. The factory for production of concrete tiles is erected in one of the refugee camps (Nazir Bagh camp). Thousands of refugees stream over the border to escape the war in Afghanistan—by the end of the year there are approximately 1.3 million (10 years later 3.5 million)

1984

Georg and Marianne move to Peshawar. Georg becomes "Assistant Director" of Shelter Now.

Friends of Georg's who lived in Lahore, Pakistan, watched with concern developments in Afghanistan and the large streams of refugees who were coming into Pakistan; they visited the refugee camps north of Peshawar. Georg, who was in India at the time to scout out a future field of operations, traveled from India to Pakistan in the spring of 1982 to visit the refugee camps with his friends. The misery of the refugees' situation moved him deeply.

They made the decision to found a relief organization for the refugees and began negotiations with the government in Islamabad. In 1983 the registration was complete and aid for the refugees was started. That was the beginning of the organization Shelter Now International.

The proposal before the government was to erect low-cost houses, financed by the UNHCR. Several thousand of these buildings were to be constructed for outpatient clinics and administrative offices and schools, as the refugee camps resembled mini-towns with 10,000 to 15,000 citizens who had to be governed. The refugees had to be registered and food distribution organized. There was a special police force in Pakistan which was responsible for law and order in the camps. Administrative offices and (later) outpatient clinics had also to be built for them by Shelter Now.

The young people from Shelter Now threw themselves into planning the production of "geodesic domes," the technical term for the simple houses. These were honeycomb-shaped buildings made of six trapeziums and six triangles standing on reinforced concrete pillars. The walls could be filled in later with mud or bricks. It was planned to construct a cement works in one of the refugee camps outside Peshawar, where the reinforced pillars could be produced.

These were to be transported to the camps and put together there as houses.

The whole enterprise was to be financed by the UNHCR; the first contract consisted of 3000 houses at a cost of nearly a million US$.

Shelter Now cement works in Nazir Bagh refugee camp

The first "geodesic domes" are erected and ready for use

An Adventurous Journey to Pakistan

Georg Taubmann: Naturally we needed HGVs (heavy goods vehicles) for this factory and for transporting the reinforced concrete beams. Our leader came to Germany at the end of 1982, contacted me and informed me that they were buying second-hand HGVs and wanted to drive them overland to Pakistan. They were short of money. We gave a few talks in and around Munich, where we shared our vision about our plans to work with Afghan refugees, and collected donations. In Munich, two old HGVs and a Unimog (an all-terrain truck) were purchased. There were four of us, of whom three were drivers.

As we had friends in Italy, we drove there first at the beginning of January and worked on the trucks for the journey ahead. Then it was onto the ferry to Greece and the long road trip to Pakistan. That turned out to be an absolutely bizarre trip. I didn't actually want to go; our civil wedding service was planned for March 11th and the following day the big wedding day celebration with my fiancée Marianne. My leader said casually, "That'll not be a problem. You'll be back by then, guaranteed." The journey went through Greece and Turkey in the bitterly cold winter, in HGVs which had no heating. In Eastern Turkey it was minus 30 degrees, the roads covered with snow and ice. In parts the roads were blocked; we had to stop or use a detour. At night the diesel froze. What now? We didn't know what to do. We looked around and saw other truck drivers lighting fires under their diesel tanks and engines. We copied them and had to be careful that we didn't set our trucks on fire.

We were continually being stopped by policemen who wanted cigarettes or bribes. We encountered HGVs sunk deep in snowdrifts or broken down by the roadside. Shortly before the border into Iran, we were tricked by the police. At the checkpoint they took our passports from us. They told the driver in the vehicle ahead of us, that they had given the passports to the driver behind him. And vice versa to the driver behind— that they had given them to the driver in front.

After driving for some minutes, one of us had a sickening feeling and asked the others about it. We had just climbed a steep mountain, so we stopped and ran back down to the police station. The patrol was just leaving! After

Georg with his friend in front of their HGV

some tough negotiations they eventually handed them over. They would probably liked to have sold them.

When we reached the Iranian border the Islamic revolution was in full swing and a war was going on between Iran and Iraq. It was total chaos. We had to drive through Iran in the midst of military tension. Again and again we were stopped by young Islamic religious guards; we had to be ready for anything. Out of sympathy, we took a group of Italian and German hippies with us, as they had been robbed by Turkish police and had no more money. They just joined our convoy. We had no telephone and I couldn't tell Marianne where I was or how I was doing. The wedding day was drawing closer.

At the border between Iran and Pakistan we battled our way through a severe sandstorm. We just about managed to get across the border. From Quetta there was a flight to Lahore, but our trucks were simply too slow to be able to reach the airport in time. We asked the hippies to let me travel ahead with them, to get me to Quetta as fast as possible. They couldn't very well say no; after all we had smuggled them through Iran and paid all the charges. Off we went, and what was the next thing they did? They got themselves drugs and, music at full blast, thundered across the desert dunes to Quetta in their two vehicles. I had to arrive in Quetta that night, because the once weekly flight to Lahore went the next morning, and if I missed it I wouldn't get to the wedding on time. High on drugs, the hippies raced through the potholes.

One of the many breakdowns en route

Then there was an almighty crack—a front wheel had fallen off. I went on in the second car to Quetta. There I had to change money and buy my ticket for Lahore. The flight left at 11, the ticket booth shut at 10. I was dancing like a cat on a hot tin roof! One of the hippies ambled off to the money-changing bureau. He returned high as a kite—he'd taken his time. At long last I had the money. I argued with the people at the ticket booth, got a ticket and raced to the airport on a rickshaw. I was wrecked, totally stressed out. But the plane was still waiting and I made it to Lahore.

The first opportunity I had to make a phone call was from a hotel in Lahore. It was a Tuesday, three days before the wedding. Marianne had made all the preparations, but had no idea how and where I was. On that Tuesday, Marianne intended to order the flowers and said to herself, *If I don't hear anything from Georg today, then I'll probably have to cancel the whole wedding.* Friends and relatives kept phoning to ask where Georg was. But Marianne had no idea and didn't even know whether I was still alive. At last the welcome news: "I have arrived in Lahore and am coming on the next flight to Germany. I'll be there on time for the ceremony."

Less than 24 hours before the civil ceremony I arrived in Braunschweig, completely exhausted, and still had to buy my wedding suit, have a shave, get my hair cut—and the first wedding guests were arriving. The following day we celebrated our church wedding in our fellowship in Braunschweig.

Two-and-a-half months later the young couple was sent out to India by their church in Braunschweig. They believed that India would be their area of service; they stayed there for barely a year.

Meantime in Peshawar, Pakistan there was a Shelter Now office and a factory, in which prefabricated concrete components were being manufactured. In 1984 Georg and Marianne moved from India to Peshawar, to support the team there. Georg became Assistant Director of Shelter Now Pakistan.

For 16 years they would live and work in Peshawar. Their two sons Daniel and Benjamin were born there. It became their home.

Georg and Marianne with their sons Daniel and Benjamin in 1988

FROM 1988 – 1990

1988
Working out from Peshawar into neighboring Afghanistan, Shelter Now begins to assist returning refugees to rebuild their villages. At this time Soviet troops are still in the country and working there is very dangerous.

1989
The Soviet troops have not succeeded in bringing the country under their control in the 1980s. After 10 years of occupation they withdraw from Afghanistan. The land is ruined, the people deeply traumatised. Statistics show that approximately 1.5 million Afghans have lost their lives.

1990
In April the sites of the Shelter Now aid projects in Nazir Bagh refugee camp are plundered and razed to the ground by Islamic extremists and refugees whom they have incited.

Some weeks later there is an assassination attempt on the life of the Shelter Now leader and his son, which they only narrowly escape. He has to leave the country. Further murder threats follow, almost all foreign workers pull out and the organization is shut down.

At the end of the year Georg returns to Pakistan with his family, to rebuild Shelter Now. He becomes leader of Shelter Now in Pakistan.

Vandalism, Destruction, the End

In 1990 in Pakistan, Shelter Now experiences a similar disaster to the one in 2001 in Afghanistan. Their large Base (factory) in one of the refugee camps near Peshawar, Nazir Bagh, is completely razed to the ground by a mob incited by Islamists. The losses amount to more than 1.5 million dollars. After the assassination attempt on the life of the then leader and his son, the organization has to be closed down. The overseas staff are discouraged and return to their home countries. The local employees lose their jobs. Shelter Now is finished!

However, back in Germany, Georg has no peace. Even before their departure for Germany, he and Marianne had decided to return to Pakistan to continue to work among the Afghan refugees, despite these deeply traumatic experiences. But they don't know how, as the projects have been destroyed and Shelter Now no longer exists.

But God speaks insistently to them and against the advice of concerned friends, Georg returns to Pakistan with his family and starts again, literally from the beginning.

In 2001 the Shelter Now projects are destroyed, the offices closed, and the staff who have not been arrested have to leave the country. Again, great damage is incurred and they lose almost everything. Shelter Now is finished for a second time! Again it is Georg who takes the initiative and, a few months after his release, gathers together those colleagues who have the courage to begin anew in Afghanistan.

Georg Taubmann: We had been caring for the Afghans for seven years in the Nazir Bagh refugee camp. Thousands of low cost houses had been manufactured and built. The initial care of the newly arrived refugees was running smoothly. Thousands of children were provided with a regular supply of milk and were able to attend school. Besides the concrete factory with a large truck repair workshop in one of the camps, accommodation specifically for widows and orphans had been erected. Other organizations had built a girls' school and a clinic with a women's section. We wanted primarily to help widows and children. For each widow, we built a house with a toilet, and a common vegetable garden was laid out for everyone. There was a playground and a center in which sewing instruction was given. And then something we would never have expected occurred.

On April 26, 1990, at the end of the fasting month of Ramadan, fanatical mullahs of a radical Islamic party came and incited the refugees against all the organizations that were caring for women and children. Pakistani authorities reported later that the mullahs threatened their listeners that Allah would not hear their prayers if they did not drive out these kaffirs/heathen and destroy their projects for women and children. After the inflammatory address Islamists stormed the relief agencies' aid projects, destroying and stealing everything they could get their hands on.

The Islamists attacked every organization that was supporting women and children, and also destroyed a girls' school. Obviously it troubled them that these poor women were being helped; they were fanatical opponents of any kind of education and training for girls. The incited refugees ransacked the widows' center and destroyed everything they found. The women disappeared. We were never able to find out what happened to them or where they were taken to. The playground was razed to the ground. Nothing remained, everything was plundered. Even the vegetable garden, which had been tended to by the widows, was ruined. Likewise the girls' school. The hospital, which had been built by an American aid organization, was attacked, but armed guards were able to hold off the attackers.

Then they took on our factory. That was a massive installation: 18 vehicles were standing there, including the ancient trucks which we had driven from Germany to Pakistan in 1983. Every vehicle was stolen and what they couldn't take with them, they set on fire. The HGV workshop, in which refugees were being trained to be HGV and vehicle mechanics, was totally looted and dismantled. What couldn't be taken was burned. We had stored 175 tons of milk powder for the children's milk distribution programme. Likewise, many tons of steel and cement for reinforced concrete beams. Everything was destroyed and ransacked. Two-thousand trees had been planted all around the massive complex, and even these were hacked down. Up to 10,000 refugees came in mobs from the neighboring refugee camp and wreaked havoc, destroying everything. More and more came. They took everything that wasn't nailed down.

It was incomprehensible vandalism. When two colleagues and I saw it a day later, we were totally stunned. Bewildered, we could not believe that the people whom we had tirelessly helped for seven years, had suddenly turned against us, simply because they had been stirred up by the fanatics. Children roaming around shouted "kaffir" (unbeliever) after us, and threw stones at us. It was so depressingly awful for me, that I never wanted to enter that place again.

After the attack on the Center in the Nazir Bagh refugee camp, the Shelter Now staff from Pakistan met with the leaders from Germany and Australia, to seek advice on how things should proceed after the destruction. The Islamists had even threatened the owner of the Shelter Now office in Peshawar and demanded that he end their contract. Only immensely persuasive powers could prevent him from doing so. They were watching the homes of our colleagues, clearly with sinister plans. Danger was in the air.

Georg Taubmann: We were discussing whether we should concentrate only on Afghanistan, as we still had a cement works there. Practically all our property in Pakistan had been pillaged and ransacked. Just as we came unanimously to this conclusion and were about to end our meeting, someone knocked on the door and our project manager from the cement factory in Afghanistan walked in. He seemed to be confused and shocked; he reported to us that he had just learned that the cement works that we had built in 1989 near Jalalabad had been ransacked and destroyed by the same Islamic fanatics. They had surrounded it, forced the workers out and, just as in Nazir Bagh, looted and taken all they could and destroyed the rest. It was inconceivable; we couldn't take it in. It sounded like a nightmare, but unfortunately it was true. Now we had lost everything. But even worse was to come. The next avalanche was approaching.

A short time later the same Islamists planned to murder our director in Pakistan. They lay in wait for him, and as he went shopping outside of Peshawar with his son, they fired at his vehicle with two Kalashnikovs. They peppered the vehicle with bullets. Miraculously neither was hurt. Anyone who saw the vehicle later could not believe it. A single shot had skimmed the father's cheek.

Afterwards, he was so traumatized that he had to leave the country. He went back to America with his family. The western staff were appalled; they left Pakistan as well. A few months later the Shelter Now office was closed down.

At that time Georg was on home leave with his family in Germany, a six-month break that they took every three years.

While there, the news of the assassination attempt and the closure of the office reached him.

Return and New Beginning

Georg Taubmann: When the attack on our leader took place, we were already on home leave. We were alarmed on hearing of the closing down of the Shelter Now office in Peshawar and the return of our overseas colleagues to their home countries. Firstly we had to process it all. We prayed a lot and thought about how to proceed.

We didn't want to give up. Despite all the disappointments, we had the impression that we should go back to Pakistan, we just didn't know how. *Maybe we can join another organization.* Marianne and I racked our brains. We sought out information. But then it was as if God told us clearly that we should rebuild Shelter Now. We had deep peace in our hearts, although it seemed impossible. Our leaders were uncertain and hesitant, as it was dangerous, indeed hopeless, and we would be alone initially. But they didn't stop me.

At the end of 1990, Georg and his family go back to Peshawar. There is very little time for the new beginning, as the Gulf War, which the USA and its allies wage against Iraq, begins in January 1991. Life for foreigners in Pakistan becomes increasingly insecure. Georg senses this tension immediately on arriving in the city. Many of the local people support Saddam Hussein and demonstrate against foreigners.

Nevertheless Georg gathers his colleagues around him again and becomes the leader of Shelter Now International. The tried and tested aid projects are rebuilt: the distribution of daily food rations to refugee families, the construction of thousands of mud houses and the erection of some clinics and schools in the camps. The UNHCR hands over responsibility for the distribution of almost all food in the camps around Peshawar to Shelter Now. Food to the value of hundreds of thousands of dollars is distributed each month. The work continues until 2005, when most of the refugees have returned to Afghanistan.

> The hounding by the Islamists and their destruction of the Shelter Now projects in Nazir Bagh camp is the main theme in Pakistani newspapers throughout the country. *Newsweek* magazine also reports the event with the title "The way Afghans say, 'Thank you.'"
>
> Soon after the attack on Shelter Now, the US Embassy puts pressure on the Pakistani Government in Islamabad to investigate thoroughly the causes of the brutal looting and destruction, and the accusations against Shelter Now.
>
> A commission examines the events in every detail, over several weeks. The result: It is officially confirmed to Shelter Now that their workers had not done anything offensive that could have justified this destruction. The organization had done excellent work. The Minister President of the North West Border Province, Mr. Sherpao, hands over to Shelter Now as compensation a check with a large sum of money and with the request that they continue the work among Afghan refugees.

FROM 1991-1993

Gulf War and Threatening Letters

The security situation at the end of 1990/beginning of 1991 becomes increasingly dangerous with more and more aggressive and tense mass demonstrations in Peshawar. The few colleagues who have decided to begin working with Georg again, feel increasingly threatened. Then the Gulf War breaks out on January 17, 1991, with a heavy bombardment of Baghdad by the US army. How is Georg to continue the work and guarantee the safety of his colleagues?

Georg Taubmann: The daily increasing mass demonstrations on the streets of Peshawar caused me anxiety. The situation for foreigners was becoming ever more dangerous, and the Pakistani security authorities were organizing heavily

1991

On January 17, 1991, the so-called Second Gulf War begins with the bombardment by the US army of Baghdad in Iraq. Georg and his team have to seek refuge in the capital city, Islamabad. When they return to Peshawar, Georg receives a death threat from a radical Islamist organization.

1992

The Afghan Communist regime is overthrown by the mujahideen. Many refugees return to Afghanistan. Shelter Now gets registered in Afghanistan as an aid organization under the new government led by President Rabbani, in order to help the returning refugees with reconstruction. At the same time, hundreds of thousands of Afghans flee the conflict around Kabul and pour over the border into Pakistan; they are cared for in camps by Shelter Now.

1993

Together with two overseas colleagues, Georg is kidnapped by highwaymen (a heavily armored criminal gang that looked for opportunities to kidnap people, steal vehicles, etc.) on the way back to Peshawar from one of their projects in Khost, Afghanistan. Through the intervention of a passing group of Pashtuns who challenged the criminals, nearly starting a deadly firefight, they escape at the last possible moment.

---

guarded convoys of foreigners to the airport. Many foreigners were leaving the city and the country.

We didn't want to leave again so soon, seeing that we had only recently started again. We just wanted to stay inside our homes and wait it out. I knew, however, what hotheaded, unrestrained masses could get up to. Suddenly, I sensed a deep unrest within. An inner voice urged me, *Leave the city at once!* A short time later, it proved to be absolutely correct. We gave our computers and other important documents from the office into the safekeeping of a trustworthy Pakistani.

I had not intended to leave the city until the following night, but I felt such a strong urgency that I ordered our colleagues, "Pack the most necessary things—don't forget your passports. We've got to leave immediately!" We secretly left the city and fled under cover of darkness to Islamabad. We arrived there at 7 o'clock in the morning, and the first thing we learned was that the Gulf War had broken out after our departure.

As a result, there were large demonstrations with violent riots in Islamabad and especially in Peshawar. Incensed crowds, ready to use violence, stormed through the city, noisily scanning the area where we lived. Our watchman told us later that some demonstrators came to our house and wanted to find out from him if we were there, where we were hiding. They were searching especially for foreigners. That was close, because we had left the house only a few hours earlier.

We had to remain for a whole week in Islamabad, before we could return. It was safer in the capital. We had hardly come back and gotten the offices into shape when a threatening letter arrived from a radical Islamist organization: I was to leave the country; they were giving me 10 days to pack my things, "otherwise we will send you to hell." This organization was already responsible for grenade attacks on the UNHCR office and an English NGO in Peshawar. It was clear that they were serious and that we were their next target.

So, only very few weeks after my return, we also had the next death threat after the attack on our organization and our former CEO. I turned to the American Consulate—the German Consulate was closed. They came to our office in an armored vehicle and had a look at the letter. "You must take this threat seriously and disappear as soon as possible," was their recommendation.

"But I have just come back. The work must be rebuilt. I don't want simply to leave again," I replied, depressed.

"Mr. Taubmann, you cannot stay!" But I insisted that I wanted to stay. After some discussion they advised, "If you are going to stay, then you must take tough security measures. The office has to be secured. You must leave for the office at different times and keep changing your route."

Naturally I was afraid. Who wouldn't have been? I consulted with Marianne, and when we prayed, we had an inner peace that we should stay.

A few days later some of our watchmen came running to our home and reported nervously that someone had tried to throw a grenade into our office. But he threw it too far and it landed in a neighbor's garden and exploded. The grenade tore a huge hole in the ground, the flak flew all over the place and did damage to our office on the other side of the wall. No one was injured.

An American employee of an overseas organization lived next door, but he was not at home. The police who took statements about the incident knew nothing of my threats and assumed that the American was the intended target. So they put up a tent directly in front of our office and set up a regular police presence. So we then had better protection as well. Again a huge obstacle had been overcome and the rebuilding of Shelter Now could continue.

Development projects in Afghanistan

In 1992 the Afghan Communist regime is overthrown by the mujahideen. Many refugees in the Pakistani camps prepare to return to their villages in Afghanistan. But everything there is destroyed and torn down. Shelter Now wants to assist the returning Afghans with reconstruction. Under life threatening conditions, they begin to build cement works for the production of material for the roofing of houses and toilets in Khost Province, and later also in Paktia Province, Jalalabad, Kandahar and Lashkargah/Helmand. In accordance with the regulations, they have themselves registered as an aid organization under the new government of President Rabbani.

Georg Taubmann: It was a terrible, chaotic time for Afghanistan, because the country was ruled by different warlords, and by mujahideen leaders of the most varied parties. Whenever we traveled from Peshawar to Kabul, Afghanistan, we had to pass through about 10 different check-posts of the most varied mujahideen groups. We were stopped and strictly checked. When we drove in HGVs with aid supplies, they demanded fees. Sometimes we even had to unload the HGVs for checking. During the Russian occupation, the main cities were protected against the mujahideen and remained largely unscathed. Now they were contested by the various mujahideen groups. In Kabul there were very serious battles for years and over this period the city was to a large extent destroyed. Kandahar was also strongly contested and ruined; it was the same in other cities. The chaos and lawlessness were dreadful, constantly escalating.

The minefields set by the Russians presented another great danger. One had to be extremely careful. Once we were driving through a village and were about to take the unpaved road which led to the next village. Suddenly the villagers shouted and ran after us. We stopped and they warned us about going farther. What we didn't know was that the road was still mined. If the stones to the right and left of a "road" were marked with red stones, it meant one should never deviate from it. That was very dangerous for everyone. Red-colored stones always meant that there were mines nearby.

Simultaneously with the reconstruction work in Afghanistan, there was a flood of refugees coming in the opposite direction from Kabul into Pakistan. The city which was conquered by the mujahideen was so fiercely attacked and destroyed that hundreds of thousands of Afghans, in many cases accused of being Communists, abandoned the city in haste and sought refuge in Pakistan. The Pakistani administration could scarcely cope with the onrush.

Georg Taubmann: At the beginning of 1993 there were again fierce battles in Kabul. It was one of the worst power struggles among the warlords. Each of them wanted to control the city. Firing went on for days. On one of the days of the ceasefire, tens of thousands fled from Kabul and headed east towards the Pakistani border.

Completely traumatized, they transported their injured and dead with them. The head of the Pakistani Refugee Authority called all the leaders of the aid agencies together and described the dramatic situation. The flood of refugees was so great that the border had to be closed. More than a hundred thousand had to camp out on the Afghan side. They weren't only traumatized, they were sick, hungry and dehydrated. It was practically impossible to care for them on the other side of the border. On the Pakistani side, a section of the crowd was led to our former factory site in Nazir Bagh that had been completely destroyed and looted—the place in which I never again in my life wanted to set foot.

Too much horror had occurred there! But then I got the strong impression that God was telling me that it was exactly where I should go, in order to help these poor people. And so I took over the responsibility for the rebuilding of new projects for essential primary care: the water tankers rolled in and a massive soup kitchen and bakery were set up. We built a mud house literally for every family who sought refuge there. These refugees were town dwellers, mostly despised as Communists, and were very poor at organizing themselves. Refugees from the villages understood how to build simple houses and dig wells.

In the middle of the camp stood our huge water tower, which the vandals hadn't managed to destroy when they razed our center to the ground in 1990. The new refugees were curious, asking what this monster was doing in the desert. When they heard the story of the destruction of the plant and the expulsion of the Christian organization Shelter Now, and were told that those very same people were now going to care for them, their admiration for us grew enormously.

Georg in front of the water tower

After the withdrawal of the Soviet Army and the collapse of the Communist regime in Kabul, many large aid organizations pulled out of Afghanistan, among them the USA state development agency (USAID). They left behind huge numbers of vehicles, office furniture, aid equipment and other materials which they placed at the disposal of the organizations who remained. Rather late in the day Georg heard about this and put in an application. He and his team were thrilled when they heard the news that their application had been accepted.

Georg was invited into the office in the massive fenced-in area of USAID, where there were many sheds and parking lots full of HGVs, private cars, excavators and machines. He went through huge storage halls with the administrator. Georg could only marvel at the abundance. The administrator gave Shelter Now everything that was on their wish-list: HGVs, cars, office furniture, air conditioners, refrigerators, desks and chairs. In the following weeks Georg received more and more phone calls from the administrator, informing him that more vehicles and other equipment had been brought into the storage sheds. Georg went there, full of anticipation, and returned with another series of vehicles and valuable objects. When Georg asked the administrator on one occasion if he had any more office equipment, he thought about it for a moment, then he remembered that a large part of the office furnishings in the main office in Peshawar had not yet been distributed.

They drove there together, went through all the office space, and he generously stuck red dots on everything he considered dispensable: office cupboards, desks and chairs, air conditioners and refrigerators.

The value of these pieces of equipment was far higher than the damages which Shelter Now had incurred during the attack on their plant in Nazir Bagh. For Georg this overwhelming experience was a sign of the care of his generous God. When he was ready to return again to the camp in Nazir Bagh, to help the new refugees, he unexpectedly got back more than had been ransacked and destroyed in April 1990.

Rescued at the Last Moment

Frequently during their work in Afghanistan, Georg and his staff were caught in conflicts between warring tribes. Once on the return trip from a newly founded factory in Khost, shortly before the border into Pakistan, they were captured by robbers who kidnapped them and were only willing to release them for a ransom. A group of passing Afghans, who fortunately recognized the explosive nature of the situation, managed to distract the kidnappers and the Shelter Now team were able to flee.

Georg Taubmann: I had once again been on a visit to our first project in the region of Khost, with two of our overseas and some Afghan colleagues. It lies in the east of Afghanistan. Scenically, it is a wild, mountainous area. The inhabitants are similarly wild. When I was there, I hardly ever saw a man without his Kalashnikov. The various Pashtun tribes who have their homes there, were at enmity with one another and fought against each other. They are also well-known for kidnapping and demanding ransoms. In this area, which was badly damaged because of the warring conflicts, we had built a concrete girder factory—as already stated, our first cement works in Afghanistan.

We were on the way back from visiting this factory. We had visited our colleagues there and also had a meeting with the governor of Khost. On the return journey from Khost to Miranshah we had to pass through an area notorious for its dangers.

Miranshah lies directly on the Afghan border. It is a very dangerous border area. We were traveling in two jeeps, our Afghan colleagues in the front jeep. The track went steeply up a mountain and we had to proceed slowly. Suddenly, a man stepped out in front of us on the road and blocked our way. We had no option; we had to stop.

The man began to converse and argue with our Afghan colleagues in the lead vehicle. In the second vehicle, we watched as the argument escalated and increased in volume and wild gestures.

Initially we were merely surprised, thinking, *Maybe he just wants a lift*. But when I looked to the right up the hill, I discovered a man with a Kalashnikov trained on us. I looked a little farther; another man with a turban and a Kalashnikov. At least four armed men had their Kalashnikovs pointed at us. We were encircled by armed men. It was clear to us, if we made a move or produced weapons, they would have shot us immediately. There was no chance of escaping. Our Afghan colleagues got out of their vehicle, and we knew there was something very threatening going on. Uneasily we slid back and forth on our seats and watched the scene.

Finally we too got out and went forward. "Tell me, what's going on here?" I asked our colleagues. "Mr. George, these are very evil men kidnapping us. They want to drag you three foreigners and us into the mountains in order to demand ransom money."

"What will we do now?" I was concerned.

"We'll try to bargain with them and appeal to their sense of hospitality and honor." And they really did. "These three foreigners are guests here in the region. Mr. George has come to help your people build their houses. You Pashtuns are renowned for your hospitality" and so on, and so on … Nothing would move them to relent. The hostile Kalashnikovs remained trained on us. The discussion became more and more heated. My heart thumping, I looked from one to the other. The interesting thing was that cars and state buses kept coming along the track and drove right past us. They recognized the dangerous situation and were intent on getting away from it.

Our heated debate had already lasted over an hour and I observed how our Afghan colleagues' nerves were becoming frayed. I too felt increasingly ill at ease. My two overseas colleagues, Greg and Steve, prayed, full of desperation, that no unpremeditated actions or words would lead to a fatal end and that we would all escape through some sort of miracle.

Finally they were just shouting at each other. I knew that we foreigners were like gold dust for the gangsters. We were in an area where there were no laws. There was of course a governor, but outside the city limits he had no power. The tribal groups did what they pleased. I saw from our Afghan colleagues that they couldn't do any more. Disappointed and discouraged, their shoulders slumped as they were once again yelled, "That's it! The foreigners are coming with us!" Hesitantly we went to our jeep, put down the car keys and took our sleeping bags and a few things from the back.

Suddenly a pick-up truck, fully loaded with Pashtuns, comes driving up the hill. A somewhat younger man with a conspicuous turban looks out of the side window and asks, "What's the matter here?"

Relieved, I answer quickly, "They're taking us with them. We're being kidnapped."

Decisively and with a certain pride he gets out of the truck; all the other Pashtuns jump down from the tailgate. They go up to the man and begin to quarrel with him. They too have their Kalashnikovs. Then it gets quite heated, they gesticulate, they fight, finally they begin to shout. I'm becoming increasingly afraid that they will start shooting at each other. It's becoming more and more dramatic.

We three foreigners stand there, praying ever more intensively that Jesus will save us out of this hopeless situation! Then I notice how they are slowly encircling the leader of the kidnappers as they debate. My eyes get bigger. One man detaches himself from the group and hisses, "Go! Go quickly! Quick, quick! Disappear!"

As quick as lightning I get into the first jeep and switch on the engine. My two friends react also. The Afghan workers dash into the second vehicle. As I start, one of the kidnappers on the hillside aims at me. He tries to establish eye contact with his encircled leader, but he doesn't yet realize what's going on. So the marksman pauses uncertainly at his post. I just disregard him. I step hard on the accelerator and race up the track. We three keep our heads down, fearing we'll be shot any minute, then breathe sighs of relief when at last we head down the mountain and we're out of shooting range. I don't take my foot off the accelerator until we reach the border post.

There we waited for the second jeep, which soon arrived. We paused for a while directly on the border, as it was safe there. Eventually the men who had rescued us drove up. We thanked them from the bottom of our hearts and exchanged addresses. Later they often visited us in Pakistan and in Afghanistan. The leader was a very courageous young man, a so-called Pir, a Sufi religious leader among the Pashtuns.

In my opinion he was a special person, who understood how to act confidently and bravely and who possessed authority. For us it was an incredible rescue. If we had been captured, I don't know what would have happened to us. Not to be contemplated! God had rescued us again out of a dangerous situation!

Khairat, a Pashtun Celebration of Thanksgiving

When I later told the Afghan workers our story, everyone who heard it said, "We must celebrate, have a Khairat!"

"What's a Khairat?" I asked. I had heard the word, but didn't know what it meant. "It's a celebration to show gratitude, which we hold in our Pashtun culture. For example, when someone has been ill and hasn't died, or has survived an attack, or has had a bad accident and survived. Or like with you: You just escaped the kidnap and possibly death," they explained. "We have a huge celebratory feast and share it with the poor. In doing so, we give thanks to God and tell our story. That's what we always do."

When I heard that, it was clear to me—we'll do it in the middle of the Nazir Bagh refugee camp, where we helped refugees right from the beginning and saved many people's lives. It was shortly before Christmas and we wanted to do something special in any case for the refugees on that occasion.

We announced the Khairat. We cooked massive amounts of rice and meat in enormous pots. As is the tradition, I had to relate my story before the feast. Everyone was waiting in anticipation. The workers had installed loudspeakers and a microphone, as many refugees had come. I got up on the back of an HGV, and the loudspeaker was on top of the driver's cabin, so that the approximately 2000 refugees who had gathered could hear me. And then I told my story. How we were on the way from Khost to Pakistan, were captured, should have been dragged off, how we had given up all hope, how we pleaded unceasingly with God for help—and suddenly this vehicle arrived with the brave men who rescued us, and we were able to escape without a hair on our heads being touched. To finish off, I raised my hands and

Georg, with a translator, tells his story from a truck to approximately 2,000 listeners

thanked God that he had sent these men to save us. Many of the listeners, including the mullah, raised their hands reverently in prayer, applauded and rejoiced. Even the worthy mullah with his white beard was delighted and enthused over this wonderful rescue story and how God had saved us.

FROM 1994-2000

1994
The Taliban who have been trained and armed in Pakistan occupy Afghanistan and after a few years are in control of almost the whole country.

1996
The capital, Kabul, is taken by the Taliban. Now the Taliban exercise power over all of Afghanistan. The next large flood of refugees into Pakistan ensues; 10,000 Afghans flee the despotic rule of the Taliban. Shelter Now is able to continue its projects unhindered, in part supported by the Taliban, at least when the Taliban ask for their help.

1998
In Kabul, Shelter Now is registered officially under Taliban rule as a humanitarian organization. Under the leadership of Len Stitt and his wife, Diane, the first workers move to Kabul and start up the office.

2000
Georg and his family move to Kabul. Kabul is largely in ruins and with many Islamists from all over the world. The city is plagued with poverty and an atmosphere of fear and oppression. Shelter Now devotes itself to the poorest of the poor with meals for street children, and cares for internal refugees in what was then the largest refugee camp in the world, in the desert outside Herat. Outpatient clinics are built and irrigation systems repaired. Five factories for concrete roof girders are put into operation.

From Mujahideen Terror to Taliban Terror

The population of Afghanistan is increasingly disappointed in the mujahideen and suffers under the constant fighting. In 1994 the Taliban suddenly appear. They compel the people in the villages and towns to join their movement and after a few years have almost the whole country under their control. Due to the lawlessness, murders, pillaging and the cruel and bloody ethnic clashes during the mujahideen rule, many Afghans long for peace and welcome the Taliban.

Their leader Mullah Omar fights the mujahideen and defeats them. The movement spreads throughout the country, until Kabul is taken by them in 1996. This is the actual beginning of Taliban rule over Afghanistan.

Interestingly, the activities of Shelter Now are not restricted by the Taliban leadership. They are welcomed, can register their organization, and their projects prosper.

Georg Taubmann: In 1996 we were even requested specifically by the Taliban to come to Kandahar and set up one of our tried and trusted cement works there. Everywhere the houses were in ruins. Using our reinforced concrete pillars, the villagers were able to erect houses for themselves and fill out the walls with mud. However there was no roofing material. In Afghanistan there is a shortage of wood and it is very expensive. We then produced cement girders and slabs that they could put on top of the walls.

In Kandahar our office was situated between Mullah Omar's headquarters and the airport, where the center of Osama bin Laden and the Al Qaeda movement was. At that time, Osama bin Laden had already accumulated thousands of fighters around him. Everywhere in the bazaar one saw Arabs who had arrived from throughout the Arab world. With the Osama bin Laden Centre in the neighborhood, we were in illustrious company! We had no idea what would happen to us in five years' time.

While the Taliban extend their dreadful rule and track down dissidents, while women have to suffer the terror of the religious police, Shelter Now is able to spread out from Kandahar to Helmand, where another concrete girder factory is built. A further factory is erected in Jalalabad on the insistence of the Taliban. In the city, the Taliban place the former buildings and grounds of the Russian KGB at their disposal. Eventually they are working in nine provinces ruled by the Taliban. Shelter Now enjoys the favor and the support of the Taliban.

Many Western organizations are irritated and uncertain whether they can or should continue to work at all under Taliban rule. Shelter Now on the other hand sets up an office in Kabul in 1998 and gets registered under their rule. A courageous step! Under the leadership of Len Stitt, the first volunteers move to Kabul and build up the organization there. Georg continues to lead the work from Peshawar. There is still lots to do in the refugee camps, and he shuttles to and fro between there and Afghanistan.

Move to Kabul and Settling In

In June of 2000, they move to Kabul as a family and settle into a new home. Greg Gilmore becomes leader of Shelter Now in Pakistan.

Though they are all looking forward to moving to Kabul, the departure affects them keenly. They have lived for a full 16 years in Peshawar. They have many Afghan, Pakistani and overseas friends whom they now have to leave behind. Daniel and Benni were born there. They have known no other home; it's where they have their closest friends—with whom they are still in touch, even today.

> Daniel was born in Peshawar, Benjamin in a mission hospital in the north of Pakistan, directly on the famous Silk Road. Benni always had difficulty explaining where he was born. Later he could say that it was quite near to Abbottabad, where Osama bin Laden was holed up when he was discovered and killed by American Special Forces.

When they get into the trucks to leave for Kabul, eyes full of tears, lots of people line the street to say their goodbyes, among them a row of beggars whom they had quietly supplied with food almost every day.

Kabul is full of Islamists from all over the world. The streets are controlled by the infamous Religious Police. Life there is dangerous for foreigners. Many organizations had left the country when the Taliban took over.

Marianne Taubmann: I found the move from Pakistan to Afghanistan really difficult, because we had to leave our friends and our accustomed environment. On the road to Kabul I wept a lot. I didn't know Afghanistan. It was all a beginning-from- zero again, whether setting up the new house, becoming oriented to the new surroundings or shopping. We had to make new contacts. A completely new start!

Kabul is a Dari-speaking city. In Peshawar we spoke Pashtu. Now I had to learn Dari. The culture was quite different too. When I envisage it now, I realise I went through a real culture shock.

Most of all, I found the ubiquitous Taliban presence strange and threatening. Our female colleagues told me that they were spat at. Others were forced to jump into the ditch by the aggressive driving style of the Taliban. When shopping I witnessed Afghan customers being beaten. I was used to driving a car myself, even in Pakistan. But for the Taliban it was unthinkable that a woman should be at the steering wheel. On one occasion I drove a short distance with the boys to another house. When I overtook a jeep with Taliban in it, I was brutally forced to the side. Their evil stares went right through me—I couldn't get it out of my head for a long time.

Going out to restaurants was no longer as relaxing as in Pakistan. Whenever we went with friends or colleagues to a restaurant, we were met with hate-filled stares from nearby Taliban or members of Al Qaeda. We would be led quickly into a side room so that we were safe from their verbal or even physical attacks.

Georg Taubmann: The Embassy of Chechnya was very near our house. Just outside Kabul there was a huge camp with thousands of Pakistanis, and generally the city was full of Islamists from all over the world who were being trained as terrorists.

Many of them lived in the area where we lived. The oppression could be felt everywhere. Sharia law prevailed. The streets were patrolled by the notorious Religious Police, who cruelly punished passers-by for the most trivial offence.

The majority of freedom-loving or wealthy Afghans had fled by this time and were living abroad. Daily life was becoming more and more intolerable. Thousands of widows were living in Kabul. Many of them had moved to Kabul during the Communist regime, as the government then had cared for them. But not the Taliban! Women were, in any case, no longer permitted to work. They sat at the edge of the road, even in the depths of winter, and begged. At the same time, hordes of begging children roamed through the streets. Our colleagues Katrin and Silke couldn't bear to see this and began a project for street children.

Shelter Now maintains aid projects in nine provinces in Afghanistan. In Herat, a new office has opened under the leadership of Len Stitt, in order to facilitate work in the largest refugee camp in the world, the Maslagh Camp. Internal refugees, who have moved there because of the continuing devastating five-year drought, live in this camp. Three-hundred-and-twenty-thousand to 350,000 have had to leave their villages and now live in a camp in the desert outside Herat, without either tents or more permanent accommodation. Some of them have dug holes in the desert earth and spread tarpaulins over them to protect themselves from the strong, continuous "120-day wind." In the exceptionally hard winter, several hundred Afghans freeze to death. The Taliban don't even have money to buy the linen shrouds and ask Shelter Now for white cloth to bury the dead according to their custom. The suffering of the population in Afghanistan is intolerable.

The United Nations imposes an embargo on Afghanistan. Aircraft may no longer fly into the country and trade is forbidden. There are now only three embassies in Kabul that maintain diplomatic relationships with the Taliban regime. Many aid agencies, which until now have persevered, finally depart.

Nevertheless, Shelter Now is continually being asked for help by the Taliban, especially with the provision of water in needy areas. Wells are again dug and winter aid programs implemented with blankets, food and firewood. The Shelter Now staff are happy to be able to support the poorest of the poor during this difficult time. Especially those who have nothing and cannot afford to flee to the camps in Pakistan.

In spite of the challenging political situation, the Shelter Now workers feel reasonably safe. Georg has good relationships, even friends among the influential Taliban leaders. He knows their language and the culture of the Pashtuns very well. The Taliban too repeatedly show their gratitude and their appreciation for the commitment of Shelter Now.

But the extremists among them are obviously asserting themselves in the background. Osama bin Laden is preparing the attack on the World Trade Center on September 11, 2001. Mullah Omar, the spiritual and political head of the Taliban, was becoming increasingly more powerful, controlling a massive portion of the country. And the Shelter Now colleagues are taken hostage.

FROM 2001-2002

2001

At the beginning of August, eight foreign Shelter Now staff and 16 national staff are arrested. The offices and current projects are ransacked and shut by the Taliban. A 105-day period of arrest follows in various prisons.

The situation for the prisoners is exacerbated by the terror attack on the World Trade Center in New York on September 11th. Now they are officially hostages. On October 7th US forces attack Afghanistan with the aim of removing the Taliban regime and rescuing the hostages.

On October 15th the Shelter Now colleagues are freed in a dramatic action by USA Special Forces helicopters. On December 6th the Taliban are finally defeated and driven out of Afghanistan.

2002

In April Georg travels to Pakistan with his family and meets colleagues who are prepared to build up the work again in Pakistan and Afghanistan.

In June Georg returns to Kabul with his family. Offices are rented and furnished. In Kabul there is a spirit of optimism. Many aid organizations offer help with reconstruction.

The project is called "Villages of Hope." It is started in the region around Shamalie. Refugees who were cared for by Shelter Now for years in Pakistan, return and rebuild their villages with the help of Shelter Now. Involvement in Pakistan increases. A new registration of Shelter Now with the goal of undertaking development projects and disaster relief is introduced.

FROM 2003-2008

2003
The Taliban, who had been driven out and had withdrawn largely into Pakistan, reappear with attacks that increase in intensity year by year.

2004
Marianne returns to Germany with the two boys. Georg remains on his own in Kabul. The team grows to 30 foreign workers, from approximately 15 nations. Years of extensive building of aid projects.

2005
Aid for Afghan refugees in Pakistan comes to an end. The last refugee camps are closed down. Now it's a matter of helping the returning Afghans to take their future into their own hands. Shelter Now registers again in Pakistan, this time as a humanitarian organization working for needy Pakistanis.

In the north of Pakistan there is a devastating earthquake. The most severe earthquake that has ever shaken this region leaves 100,000 dead. Shelter Now is among the first aid organizations to distribute aid in the affected areas and to help with rebuilding.

Further development or projects in Afghanistan

2007
In the first instance a project with a nomadic people group, the Kutchis, is started. They are provided with foodstuff and sheep for breeding, so that they can support themselves.

2008
The training project for fruit growing in the province of Herat is called "Trees of Hope." The project "Saffron instead of Opium," built up by two German agriculturalists, helps wean farmers away from opium cultivation and to earn their living from valuable saffron.

FROM 2008-2014

2008

In February and March there are two kidnap attempts on Georg, which he escapes. Georg takes precautionary measures and remains in the country, as a change in leadership is, in any case, to take place in July.

In July Georg moves to Germany to set up the International Shelter Now office in Sulzbach-Rosenberg, his hometown. Through Georg's efforts and further worldwide lecture tours new offices are opened in Holland, England and Australia, and workers drawn in from all over the world.

2009

In the West of Afghanistan a dental clinic is erected; it is seen as the most modern in the whole country.

Farmers receive micro-loans to purchase a cow and so can increase their herd of cattle.

In Kabul Shelter Now takes over a primary school and in the northeast they support an orphanage and offer technical training. The same thing happens in a centre for the deaf.

2010

The people in Northern Pakistan suffer a huge flood disaster. Again Shelter Now can respond quickly and effectively.

2014

"Honey is medicine" they say in Afghanistan. Families are equipped with beehives and are instructed on how to produce and market honey.

FROM 2014-2018

New Relief and Development work started in Northern Iraq (Kurdistan)

2014

ISIS conquers large swathes of Iraq and rules with extreme brutality, very similar to the Taliban in Afghanistan.

In August hundreds of thousands of people flee into the autonomous region of Kurdistan in the north of the country. Those most directly affected are Christians and Yezidis.

New possibilities open up for Shelter Now to provide humanitarian work among the refugees in Kurdistan begins. Through local partners, nutrition, hygiene articles, winter clothing, small radiators, drinking water and water filters are distributed. Children are provided with school materials, mobile clinics and a wholesale bakery are supported.

2015

The ISAF withdraws from Afghanistan. Afghan troops *are* still being trained by NATO units, but should be taking over the task of protecting the nation on their own. Large areas come under Taliban rule; they soon control over 60% of the whole country.

There are only a few aid agencies that continue to work amidst the many dangers.

2016

The provincial capital of Herat gets a teaching clinic for dentistry. Cooperation with the university is a new dimension. Students are offered practical training courses. A school dental program is initiated.

2018

The security situation has become increasingly dangerous also for Shelter Now and expats from all the other organizations. In Kabul 10 foreign staff undertake administrative work for the projects. They cannot visit many of the projects outside Kabul, which are administered by responsible and independent Afghan colleagues.

Today: Despite all these challenges, the staff members of SNI, with the help of Jesus, continue their work with great dedication and commitment to the people of Afghanistan. Despite the war and many dangers, they work and are supporting projects in at least eight provinces of Afghanistan, carrying out more than 30 development and relief projects. They even have plans to increase their humanitarian help throughout the country.

Endnotes

1. "Shelter Now International" will henceforth be shortened to "Shelter Now" throughout the balance of the book. The name "Shelter" bears testimony to the philosophy of the Aid Organization: Christian love of one's neighbor means both to feed the poorest of the poor and also to provide a roof over their head.

2. In the original version of the book *Escape from Kabul* (2002), Georg described their release on the urgent request of the US Special Forces in a slightly modified form. In order not to endanger the undertaking of further release efforts and to protect the bearer of the satellite phone, scenes had to be shifted and details withheld. Now enough years have passed so that you can read the true story in this edition.

3. The *salwar kameez* is a two-piece Arab garment, consisting of a long shirt and comfortable wide trousers.

4. ISAF = International Security Assistance Force; see p.76

5. At Easter 2000, I (the author) was on a visit to Georg in Peshawar with my family. We were in a cross-country vehicle (four-by-four) on an outing to the Khyber Pass, when Georg received a call from his project leader. Sitting in the passenger seat, I was able to follow the conversation. "Mr. George, we have just received a request from the UN, if we can take on the provision of initial care for refugees from Shamalie in Afghanistan. Several

thousand have crossed the border and are being accommodated here in a camp." "Yes, we can do that," Georg replied. "Send off our water tankers immediately with fresh drinking water, and whatever flat bread you can find. Tomorrow I'll drive to the camp and see what else is needed." *Wow*, I thought, *aid can be given so fast and so simply.*

The next morning we had the opportunity to go and see the refugee camp with Georg. The refugees were provided for from that day on, till they were able to return to Afghanistan in 2002. These were the same refugees that SNI (Shelter Now International) helped later to rebuild their destroyed villages in Shamilie.

6   This project was built with financial aid from the German Government and the German organization "Nehemia."

7   This project was accomplished by Children in Need together with Shelter Now.

www.ingramcontent.com/pod-product-compliance
Lightning Source LLC
Chambersburg PA
CBHW061258110426
42742CB00012BA/1964